THE BEDFORD SERIES IN HISTORY AND CULTURE

Herodotus and Sima Qian: The First Great Historians of Greece and China

A Brief History with Documents

Related Titles in
THE BEDFORD SERIES IN HISTORY AND CULTURE
Advisory Editors: Lynn Hunt, *University of California, Los Angeles*
David W. Blight, *Yale University*
Bonnie G. Smith, *Rutgers University*
Natalie Zemon Davis, *Princeton University*
Ernest R. May, *Harvard University*

Spartacus and the Slave Wars: A Brief History with Documents
Translated, Edited, and with an Introduction by Brent D. Shaw, *University of Pennsylvania*

Augustus and the Creation of the Roman Empire: A Brief History with Documents
Ronald Mellor, *University of California, Los Angeles*

Mao Zedong and China's Revolutions: A Brief History with Documents
Timothy Cheek, *University of British Columbia*

Herodotus and Sima Qian: The First Great Historians of Greece and China

A Brief History with Documents

Thomas R. Martin

College of the Holy Cross

BEDFORD/ST. MARTIN'S   Boston   ♦   New York

For Bedford/St. Martin's

Publisher for History: Mary V. Dougherty
Director of Development for History: Jane Knetzger
Senior Editor: Heidi L. Hood
Developmental Editor: Debra Michals
Editorial Assistant: Jennifer Jovin
Production Assistant: Samuel Jones
Executive Marketing Manager: Jenna Bookin Barry
Project Management: Books By Design, Inc.
Index: Books By Design, Inc.
Text Design: Claire Seng-Niemoeller
Cover Design: Richard DiTomassi
Cover Art: Herodotus: *Marble bust of Herodotos*. Roman, Imperial, 2nd century AD.
    Marble, Island? H. 18¾ in. (47.6 cm). The Metropolitan Museum of Art, Gift of
    George F. Baker, 1891 (91.8). Image © The Metropolitan Museum of Art. Sima Qian:
    From *Shi Ji*. Online at <http://www1.chinaculture.org/created/2005-11/29/
    content_76447.htm>.
Composition: TexTech International
Printing and Binding: RR Donnelley & Sons Company

President: Joan E. Feinberg
Editorial Director: Denise B. Wydra
Editor in Chief: Karen S. Henry
Director of Marketing: Karen R. Soeltz
Director of Editing, Design, and Production: Marcia Cohen
Assistant Director of Editing, Design, and Production: Elise S. Kaiser
Manager, Publishing Services: Emily Berleth

Library of Congress Control Number: 2009928648

For information, write: Bedford/St. Martin's, 75 Arlington Street,
Boston, MA 02116   (617-399-4000)

ISBN-10: 0-312-41649-0
ISBN-13: 978-0-312-41649-2

Foreword

The Bedford Series in History and Culture is designed so that readers can study the past as historians do.

The historian's first task is finding the evidence. Documents, letters, memoirs, interviews, pictures, movies, novels, or poems can provide facts and clues. Then the historian questions and compares the sources. There is more to do than in a courtroom, for hearsay evidence is welcome, and the historian is usually looking for answers beyond act and motive. Different views of an event may be as important as a single verdict. How a story is told may yield as much information as what it says.

Along the way the historian seeks help from other historians and perhaps from specialists in other disciplines. Finally, it is time to write, to decide on an interpretation and how to arrange the evidence for readers.

Each book in this series contains an important historical document or group of documents, each document a witness from the past and open to interpretation in different ways. The documents are combined with some element of historical narrative—an introduction or a biographical essay, for example—that provides students with an analysis of the primary source material and important background information about the world in which it was produced.

Each book in the series focuses on a specific topic within a specific historical period. Each provides a basis for lively thought and discussion about several aspects of the topic and the historian's role. Each is short enough (and inexpensive enough) to be a reasonable one-week assignment in a college course. Whether as classroom or personal reading, each book in the series provides firsthand experience of the challenge—and fun—of discovering, recreating, and interpreting the past.

Lynn Hunt
David W. Blight
Bonnie G. Smith
Natalie Zemon Davis
Ernest R. May

Preface

When and where did history writing begin, in a form and with a complexity that historians today would credit as "history" worthy of the name? Could it have been as long ago as ancient Greece in the fifth century BCE with the writings of Herodotus (ca. 484–ca. 414 BCE) and early imperial China in the second century BCE with the writings of Sima Qian (ca. 145–ca. 86 BCE)? Is it likely to have sprung up independently in both places? And if it did, what were the most important similarities and differences in these independent acts of writing history?

This book supplies evidence that helps pose—and at least partially answer—these questions in a useful way. To do so, it compares representative excerpts from *The Histories* of Herodotus and *The Records of the Historian* of Sima Qian. This volume makes the case that these historians did in fact do history writing at a level that earns them the titles the first great historian of Greece and the first great historian of China. Comparing their work allows us to see more clearly what is distinctive about each one and also what is similar. It enables us to determine the common features in the ways these writers analyzed the past and the different methods each selected for indicating the significance of historic events and the actions and motivations of individuals. Finally, their writings reveal something of the civilizations in which they lived.

The books that Herodotus and Sima Qian wrote changed how their respective civilizations approached the writing of history. A comparison of their works reveals that they both viewed knowledge of the past as much more complicated than events arranged in chronological order. Above all, they recognized that no matter how objective a historian might strive to be, information about the past always needs interpretation to be understood. Furthermore, both evidently believed that making judgments in their written works about what people did in the past could provide an important guide to how people should live in the present.

This book begins with an introduction that outlines the circumstances under which these historians did their groundbreaking work. It explores why their books were so important and describes how their histories compare in scope, organization, and purpose. It stresses the ways in which these historians expected their audiences to be actively engaged in making connections between different parts of their sprawling histories. The introductory essay also explores how Herodotus and Sima Qian combined an objective approach to evidence with a subjective interpretation of events and the motivations of individuals. In addition, the introduction explains how both historians attributed a moral value to the study of history.

The second part of the book features translated documents excerpted from *The Histories* and *The Records of the Historian*. The selections were chosen to illustrate the writers' lively storytelling and the vast scope and complex structure of their histories. The excerpts from Herodotus (Documents 1–6) are presented first only because he wrote earlier than Sima Qian. All the documents are presented in the order in which they appear in the original works, except for Document 7 (Sima Qian's autobiographical letter to Ren An), which is placed before the excerpts from *The Records of the Historian* (Documents 8–14) to give readers a sense of who Sima Qian was.

To provide specific context and help identify issues for discussion and writing, each document begins with a brief headnote. Maps have been included for geographical context. The first map illustrates ancient Greece during the time of the Persian Wars, while the second map offers a look at the composition of China during the rule of the Qin dynasty. The appendixes provide additional tools for understanding the eras in which Herodotus and Sima Qian lived and worked. These include chronologies of major events relevant to the lives and works of both historians, a list of questions to facilitate classroom discussion and analysis of the documents, and a bibliography of suggested reading for further information and research.

A NOTE ABOUT THE TEXT

Ivy Sui-yuen Sun and I translated all of the documents in this volume. The translations of Documents 1–6 are based on the Greek text of the Oxford University Press third edition of *The Histories* by K. Hude (Oxford, U.K., 1927). The translation of Document 7 is based on the Chinese text of the Zhong Hua Shu Ju edition of *The Records of the Historian* by the Zhong Hua Shu Ju Editorial Board (Hong Kong, 1970). The translations of Documents 8–14 are based on the Chinese text of the Zhong Hua Shu Ju edition of *The Records of the Historian* by Gu Jiegang et al. (Hong Kong, 1959).

Our aim in translating these texts was to render readable, rather than rigidly literal, versions, while also being as faithful to the original texts as possible. Where readings in the original texts were unclear, we used our own best judgment in deciding how to translate them rather than follow any single edition's renditions. In rendering proper names, we tried to be as clear and consistent as possible. For "Herodotus," for example, we used the "us" instead of "os" ending because this seems to be a more familiar version of the name. We tried to be consistent in representing the sometimes complex structure of Chinese names, especially those with multiple syllables, but we recognize that there are other ways this could be done. We used the Pinyin system of Romanization in transliterating Chinese.

I created the titles for the documents based on the nature of the material in them. These titles were not part of the original texts.

ACKNOWLEDGMENTS

Thanks are owed to Alex Sun, Sally Sun, Hugo Sun, and Shirley Sun for consultation on the translations from Chinese. The support of the editorial team at Bedford/St. Martin's was instrumental in producing this book. Special gratitude goes to Heidi Hood, as well as to Mary Dougherty, Jane Knetzger, Jennifer Jovin, and Emily Berleth. I am also grateful to copyeditor Barbara Jatkola and Nancy Benjamin at Books By Design for help with the final stages of production. The comments of the reviewers were valuable and welcome: Alix Alixopolos, Santa Rosa Junior College; Craig Benjamin, Grand Valley State University; Mark W. Chavalas, University of Wisconsin–La Crosse; Derek Heng, Oklahoma State University; Roy Hopper, University of Memphis; Timothy Howe, St. Olaf College; Marnie Hughes-Warrington, Macquarie University; Susan Mattern-Parkes, University of Georgia. Above all, warm appreciation is due to my developmental editor, Debra Michals, for her unstinting editorial work under adverse circumstances.

Thomas R. Martin

Contents

Herodotus and Sima Qian: The First Great Historians of Greece and China

A Brief History with Documents

PART ONE

Introduction: Inventing History Writing in Greece and China

History writing in the modern sense can be traced back to ancient Greece and China. Herodotus, who wrote in the fifth century BCE, was the first great historian of Greece and therefore the Western world, and Sima Qian, who wrote in the late second/early first centuries BCE, was the first great historian of China and therefore the East. They were not the first writers from their civilizations to record the past. But they rank as the first great historians because they composed books so long and wide-ranging, so innovative in their form and content, and so remarkable in their expression of moral judgments and interpretations that they changed the way the past was presented and evaluated in their cultures and beyond.

Herodotus and Sima Qian set a new standard for history writing by conducting extensive research so that they could present an account of the past that was as objective—or based on facts and lacking in hidden bias—as possible. At the same time, their works show how difficult it can be to reconcile the often conflicting evidence about events and people's motivations for their actions. Consequently, they demonstrate that historians can be concerned with both providing an objective presentation of evidence and expressing moral judgments about the past and its lessons for the present. The term *moral judgments* in this case refers to the historian's indirect or direct evaluation of whether people's actions were good or bad. Herodotus and Sima Qian

1

show that historians, in the course of their work, inevitably create subjective—or personal—interpretations of the past.

The ancient Greeks and the ancient Chinese had no knowledge of each other's history writing. For this reason, a comparison of the histories of Herodotus and Sima Qian is really a comparison of innovations made independently by historians living and writing under different circumstances, with different cultural backgrounds, and during vastly different historical times. Although there are variations in their history writing, the similarities between their works are significant because they reveal insights into the nature of history writing that transcend cultural, geographic, political, and chronological boundaries. Therefore, a cross-cultural analysis of Herodotus and Sima Qian enables us to see the way historians might discover common themes—perhaps even universals—in human thought and conduct in the writing of history. Taken together, these first great historians also shed light on the continuing issue of how concerns for objectivity and subjectivity operate in history writing.

THE LIFE OF HERODOTUS (CA. 484–CA. 414 BCE)

The limited information we have about Herodotus's life comes from a few comments he makes in his work and from other Greek and Roman writers. Herodotus was a Greek from Halicarnassus, a town on the southwestern coast of what is today Turkey. As an international port, Halicarnassus was home to a diverse population speaking different languages and practicing different customs, with a constant stream of foreigners passing through. Herodotus therefore grew up interacting with people from many cultural backgrounds. This experience taught him that "barbarians" (the Greeks' term for people who spoke other languages), like Greeks, could be intelligent or stupid, brave or cowardly, honorable or despicable.

In the early fifth century BCE, Halicarnassus was controlled by a ruler whose power depended on support from the Persian Empire, a superpower located in what is today Iran. Herodotus's life changed forever when his family's opposition to this Persian-controlled regime forced him to flee his homeland as a young man (the precise date is unknown). Being forced into exile in the ancient Greek world usually meant a loss of status and increased hardship, and there is little evidence suggesting how Herodotus supported himself as a refugee. He began working on his history at an unknown date sometime after going into exile. It is possible that he earned money by speaking to paying audiences, who came to be entertained and educated by selections from his history that he read aloud.

The two long and brutal wars that marked the opening and the closing years of Herodotus's life inspired him to question why individuals and political states succeeded or failed and whether justice mattered in determining their fates. In the first war, today called the Persian Wars (499–479 BCE; see Map 1), a Persian army twice invaded Greece to avenge what the Persian ruler believed had been a treacherous attack by Greeks on his allies. Some Greek states surrendered to the invading force, but others, despite their usual hostility to one another, formed an alliance to fight the enemy. Though badly outnumbered by the Persians, this temporary Greek alliance defeated the invaders and drove them out of Europe (Document 4). The victory by the underdog Greeks was an overwhelming surprise to everyone, including the Persians (whose empire was not seriously weakened by this failure to capture Greece).

The war at the end of Herodotus's life, today called the Peloponnesian War (431–404 BCE), was a war of Greeks fighting Greeks: the Spartans and their allies against the Athenians and their allies. The Spartans won by striking a deal with Persia for financial support to overcome Athens's initial advantage in troops, warships, and money. Herodotus probably died before the end of the Peloponnesian War, but he lived long enough to realize that unexpected events in the course of the war meant that the Athenians, who had been confident of victory at the start, were unlikely to win. The surprising results of the two most important wars of the fifth century BCE probably influenced Herodotus to seek the deep-seated causes of events when writing history.

Herodotus spent much of his life traveling to learn more about the world. He mentions that he visited many places around the Mediterranean, voyaged far up the Nile River in Egypt, circled the Black Sea, and even ventured as far as Babylon in what is now Iraq. Everywhere he went, he asked questions about the history and customs of the various peoples he encountered, the buildings and works of art he saw, the documents he read, and the tales and legends he heard. Making inquiries, recording the answers, evaluating the likelihood that they were true, and presenting his account for others to judge—these were Herodotus's tasks as a historian informed by firsthand knowledge of his world.

Map 1. *The Persian Wars, 499–479 BCE*

In 490 BCE, the Persian king Darius sent a military expedition to punish Athens and Eretria for having helped the Ionian Greeks in their failed revolt against Persian control. The Athenians defeated this force in the Battle of Marathon, which became a symbol of Athenian courage and love of political freedom. Darius's son Xerxes invaded Greece with a massive force in 480 BCE. He defeated three hundred Spartans at the Battle of Thermopylae but returned home after losing the Battle of Salamis. The rest of his army was defeated in 479 BCE at the Battles of Plataea and Mycale, ending the Persian threat to mainland Greece.

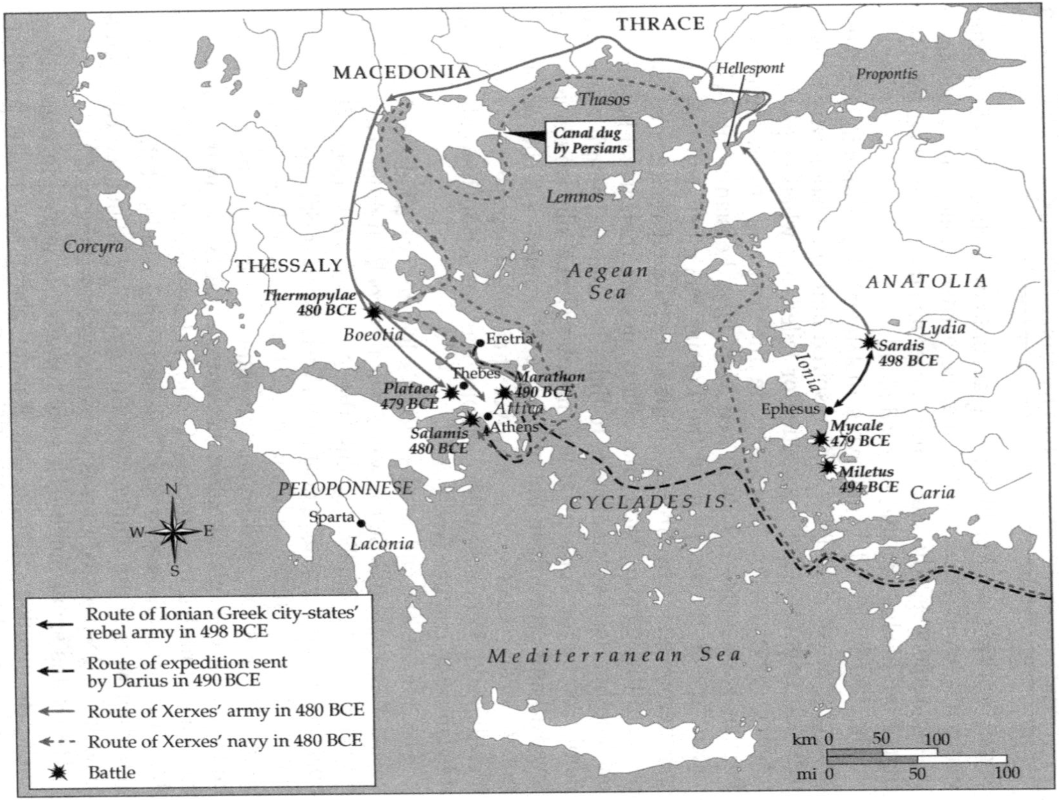

HERODOTUS'S HISTORICAL WORK: *THE HISTORIES*

Herodotus's work is today called *The Histories* (or *The History*); we do not know if Herodotus himself gave it a title. This modern title is taken from the Greek word for "inquiry" (*historie* or *historia*; see Document 1), which Herodotus uses to summarize his goals in writing history: "This is the presentation of the inquiry of Herodotus of Halicarnassus, which he presents so that what human beings have done will not fade through the passage of time and so that the great and amazing actions of the Greeks and the barbarians [non-Greeks] will not lose their fame, and in particular the reason why they went to war against one another."

A *histôr* (historian) was originally someone who collected the information necessary to serve as an impartial judge of conflicting accounts of events or as an arbitrator to settle disputes between people. A *histôr* asked questions, uncovered evidence, decided between conflicting stories, and, when appropriate, assigned responsibility and blame. A *histôr* also recognized that other people would in turn judge the correctness of his account of what happened. Herodotus therefore expected his audience to form their own judgments about what he reported.

GREEK HISTORY WRITING BEFORE HERODOTUS

The oldest works that Greeks considered to be sources of information about the past were Homer's epic poems from the eighth century BCE, *The Iliad* and *The Odyssey*. These long poems were originally preserved as oral, not written, literature. The poems, which were written down by the sixth century BCE, describe events at the time of the Trojan War, some four hundred years before Homer. The myths (from the Greek word for "stories") in *The Iliad* and *The Odyssey* served as the ancient Greeks' earliest version of history. Homer said that the Muses (goddesses of the creative arts) inspired him to record everything narrated in his works, including his stories of gods appearing in human form on earth and playing direct roles in determining the outcomes of human events from love affairs to battles.

In the sixth century BCE, Greeks in Ionia took history writing in a new direction, away from poetry and myth and toward a method based on rationality and objectivity. Contact with the intellectual achievements of other peoples, such as the work in astronomy and mathematics of the Babylonians in Mesopotamia (today Iraq), helped fuel this process in Ionia. The Ionian thinkers in science, philosophy, and religion promoted the shift away from the Greek mythological approach to history because they believed that explanations had to be based on inquiry, proven evidence, and logical reasoning to be valid. Just because a story was old or many people believed it did not make it true, they insisted. For them, Homer's myths could not be accurate history. Ionian historians wrote prose instead of poetry and did not cite the Muses as their sources. They conducted firsthand research into the past by seeking evidence and collecting information through travel.

The works of these Ionian historians have not survived, but we know that these writers focused on exploring mythology, geography, the customs of barbarians, and local histories and on developing chronologies. First, Ionian prose writers inquired into the accuracy of mythology, especially myths about the family trees of famous people who claimed that their ancestors were the offspring of sexual unions between gods and humans. The writers usually explained such myths as distorted and exaggerated versions of purely human events. When treating geography, they believed that an accurate description of the earth required eyewitness inquiry, and so they studied the accounts of travelers to learn about foreign regions and peoples. In writing about the customs of barbarians, these writers sought firsthand information about non-Greek-speaking peoples in an attempt to ascertain which customs were most beneficial for all people. They also believed that before anyone could write a large-scale history covering the entire Greek world, the writer needed to conduct focused inquiries about local histories, especially the founding of cities. Finally, these writers realized that accurate history depended on an exact reckoning of time, and hence they created works to establish chronologies, including lists of kings, top city magistrates, and religious officials. This was not easy to achieve in a world where there was no universal dating system and every location had its own calendar and way of labeling years. Although these Ionian thinkers criticized traditional stories about the gods, they acknowledged the validity of religion and the existence of divine power. In fact, they looked for better ways to understand the role of the divine in the world, often devising explanations that stressed providence as the organizing principle of the cosmos.

The most famous Ionian historian was Hecataeus, from the town of Miletus. Probably born about fifty years before Herodotus, Hecataeus wrote *Journey around the World* and *Genealogies* (or *Family Trees*), works that have survived only in scattered quotations found in the writings of later authors. *Journey* described the geography a traveler would have encountered by sailing around the Mediterranean and

Black seas and by making inland trips into southern Russia, North Africa, Egypt, Nubia, Persia, and India. In this work, Hecataeus tried to cover as much of the world as possible. This desire for comprehensive, worldwide knowledge was one of the important intellectual changes Ionian thinkers introduced.

Hecataeus's *Genealogies* revealed another change: a skeptical attitude toward traditional myths about the gods. He used logical reasoning to debunk myths that families told about their allegedly divine ancestors, explaining them away as exaggerations of ordinary events or misunderstandings of stories that were meant as metaphors rather than literal truths. Hecataeus announced his method in the first words of *Genealogies*: "Hecataeus of Miletus tells this version. I am writing what I judge to be true, because the accounts of the Greeks are many and, as they seem to me, ridiculous."[1] He understood that his role as a *histôr* was to question traditional versions of the past based on research and to present an objective account for others to judge.

THE FORM AND CONTENT OF HERODOTUS'S HISTORICAL WORK

Herodotus's groundbreaking work earned him such fame that Cicero, the distinguished Roman politician and scholar, called him "the father of history."[2] Herodotus's innovations took Greek history writing to an unprecedented level, as seen in the length and complexity of his narrative and in his objectivity in presenting historical evidence for his readers to judge for themselves. At the same time, he expressed, directly and indirectly, his own subjective interpretations of the forces driving history.

Length and Complexity of the Narrative

Herodotus's book was long—it would have filled thirty scrolls, stretching three hundred feet total—so that he could include a greater variety of topics than in previous historical writing. He covered war, politics, religion, commerce, geography, climate, ethnography, and the spectrum of individual human motivations, from cruelty and lust to generosity and loyalty.

---

[1]This quotation from Hecataeus is preserved in a much later work by Demetrius, *On Style*, sec. 12.

[2]Cicero, *On the Laws*, bk. 1, sec. 1.5.

Later editors divided Herodotus's text into the nine "books" that serve as the main divisions in modern editions. We do not know whether Herodotus wanted his text formally chunked into such sections, but it does fall naturally into two parts of roughly equal length. The first (books 1–4) describes how the Persian Empire came into existence in Iran around the middle of the sixth century BCE and grew into a superpower. The second (books 5–9) describes first the conflict in the 490s BCE between the Greek settlements in what is today western Turkey and the Persian Empire, and second the Persian invasions of the Greek mainland in the Persian Wars.

A distinctive feature of the first part of Herodotus's work is the ethnography he provides—descriptions of other, non-Greek peoples, including their customs, the geography of their lands, their temples, their buildings, and their achievements (Document 2). Herodotus's desire to understand and appreciate other cultures seems to foreshadow an important trend in modern history writing. In this context, it is also noteworthy that Herodotus reports on significant actions by women, especially among non-Greeks (Documents 1, 5, and 6). Herodotus clearly understood that gender relations are central to the ways in which human beings organize their world, with sometimes separate and other times overlapping roles for men and women. In his time, men were generally regarded as courageous and strong, while women were seen as less brave and prone to excessive erotic passion. Society valued women as mothers, daughters, and wives but blocked them from participation in politics. Women controlled the domestic space of the household and played important roles in religious activities. By highlighting women's capacities for action and influence beyond their usually restricted roles, Herodotus encouraged his audience to question preconceptions about traditional gender roles and to recognize the limitations of them.

The great length of Herodotus's book gave him room to present the complicated nature of history as he saw it. He did not write his history in strict chronological order or region by region. Instead, his narrative moves around in time and space in a nonlinear fashion and includes many stories that some critics have called irrelevant digressions. Modern scholars disagree about whether Herodotus is an unfocused storyteller who sometimes wanders away from his main subject to include odd and unreliable tidbits of information, or whether he is a subtle and sophisticated historian who expects his audience to work at understanding the connections between, and the deeper meanings of, his extensive and diverse stories.

Scholars also disagree about how to explain Herodotus's narrative complexity. Some have argued that Herodotus composed his work by putting together twenty-eight different sections, each based on different sources and having different thematic emphases. Others believe that Herodotus's work is unified by themes carried throughout. What seems clear is that Herodotus devised an intricate structure for his narrative on both a small and a large scale. Most strikingly, he uses what scholars call "ring composition." This technique involves structuring information so that a theme, event, or person that comes first in a story also appears at the end of the story, an element that comes second appears in the next-to-last place in the story, and so on. Consider, for example, Herodotus's story of the revenge of Hermotimus (Document 5). It begins with Hermotimus as a successful man, proceeds to the castration performed by Panionius willingly and then unwillingly, and ends with Hermotimus again being "successful"—at least in terms of taking revenge.[3]

Ring composition can also be seen by looking at the book as a whole. Notice first the statement at the beginning (Document 1) about Greeks and barbarians going to war "against one another." Compare that with the statement at the end of the book (Document 6) about not living as slaves "to other people." These statements, made prominent by Herodotus's ring composition, literally frame his work by pointing to a theme that is central to his narrative: how "we" interact with and relate to those whom we regard as "others." Herodotus's respect for non-Greeks and their cultural norms was unusual in ancient Greece and Rome. Five hundred years later, the philosopher Plutarch, living in the Roman Empire, still criticized Herodotus for being too favorable to barbarians.

Later Greek historians did not follow the model of Herodotus's narrative, generally writing their books in chronological order. They also criticized his method and questioned his accuracy. Thucydides of Athens, the next great Greek historian, included Herodotus when he criticized historians who dealt with events so ancient that they should remain in the realm of myth. Ctesias, a Greek from the late fifth century BCE who worked as a doctor at the Persian royal court and wrote a history of Persia, bitterly criticized Herodotus as untrustworthy.

---

[3]This is only the top level of ring composition in this story. Lack of space prevents a more in-depth analysis here, but studying the passage closely will reveal other ring compositional elements.

The most serious modern criticism of Herodotus has centered on his so-called digressions, which on the surface can seem like irrelevant folktales or weird made-up stories that are not directly related to the history of the Persian Empire or the wars between Greeks and Persians. For example, critics point to stories such as the one about skeletons that Herodotus said he saw in Arabia and that people there told him were the bones of winged snakes that flew to Egypt on annual migrations;[4] the one about ants in India that were bigger than foxes and churned up gold dust as they dug their nests;[5] and the one about cows in Africa whose horns were so large that they had to walk backward as they ate grass to avoid getting their horns stuck in the ground.[6]

Some scholars argue that this criticism reveals a misunderstanding of Herodotus's method and the goals of his complex narrative. Herodotus clearly states that amazing stories are important as pointers to the complexity of the world and of people's reactions to its often baffling nature. He also explains that his alleged digressions are in fact useful supplements that clarify or deepen themes in his main narrative. Consider, for example, the passage in book 4, section 30, that critics often cite as a fanciful tale and an apparently irrelevant digression. Here Herodotus tells a brief story about the region of Greece called Elis, where it was impossible to breed mules (the hybrid offspring of horses and donkeys). He expresses amazement at this story because, he remarks, there was no obvious natural reason, such as climate, to account for this odd situation. In explaining why he includes this story, Herodotus does not say, as some modern critics wrongly translate his remarks, that he is making a digression. What he actually says is that he finds the story "amazing," a criterion that makes it worthy of inclusion according to the goals he announces at the beginning of his book (Document 1). He also says that his method (*logos*) "has sought out supplements from the beginning." This is a crucial point for understanding Herodotus's historical method: that is, the kind of stories that some modern critics have labeled "digressions" are actually what Herodotus regarded as "supplements." Supplemental stories do just what the name implies: they supply additional—and valuable—information, such as the context, background, and underlying beliefs that enrich readers' understanding.

---

[4] Herodotus, *The Histories*, bk. 2, sec. 75.
[5] Ibid., bk. 3, sec. 102.
[6] Ibid., bk. 4, sec. 183.

Herodotus wanted his audience to do their own thinking to discover the value of such supplemental information. In this story, for example, it is crucial to note his remark that the people of Elis believed there was a curse preventing the conception of these hybrid animals within the borders of Elis. Instead, they always took their horses over the border into a neighboring region to mate them with donkeys (a behavior that inevitably meant no mules were conceived in Elis, making that part of the story true). This remark can be seen as evidence that people's belief in supernatural powers, such as the power of a curse, can be so strong that they may be willing to change their daily lives to accommodate this belief (in this case, going to huge trouble to breed mules outside their borders).

This observation about human behavior is certainly relevant to a better understanding of the conflict between Greeks and Persians, especially in comprehending why the usually disunited Greeks would band together to oppose the Persian invaders. In other words, Herodotus uses his supplements to suggest connections to larger themes in his history and expects his audience to uncover the links for themselves. That the supplements are amazing stories was also important to Herodotus, because he believed that strange and unexpected information could serve to remind people that their knowledge of the world was terribly incomplete and that they should be careful about making generalizations.

Objectivity of Evidence and Subjectivity of Interpretation

In *The Histories*, Herodotus gives his audience the responsibility of identifying connections between the many different stories in his narrative. He does this because he wants to be objective in presenting the vast evidence he has gathered from personal observation, oral stories, written accounts, inscriptions, architectural monuments, and works of art. His objectivity leads him to be open about the difficulty of evaluating the truth of what he has heard and read while doing his research. The opening sections of his book following the preface make this point clearly.[7] There he reports that the Persians and the Phoenicians (a people living on the eastern coast of the Mediterranean Sea) told conflicting versions of the famous story of the journey from Europe to

---

[7]Ibid., bk. 1, secs. 1–5.

Asia of the young Greek woman Io, disagreeing as to whether she was kidnapped or ran away voluntarily. Herodotus explicitly refuses to say which version is true. Instead, he reports the evidence from the conflicting sources and leaves it to his audience to draw their own conclusions.

At the same time, however, Herodotus presents his own subjective interpretations of the forces driving history. This recognition that historians necessarily combine objectivity and subjectivity in doing their work is another characteristic of Herodotus that seems to anticipate modern approaches to and controversies about how to write history. Forces in history that Herodotus emphasizes are the human desire for freedom, the flawed nature of human understanding of the world, and the possibility that events are determined at some deep level by the cosmic justice of *tisis* (divine retribution or vengeance). Tisis, he suggests, tends over the long term to compensate for excesses in human behavior, thereby achieving a rough justice in the workings of the world. Sometimes this cosmic justice amounts to punishment, especially when humans behave in ways that bring *nemesis* (divine retaliation) upon themselves or their descendants, as in the stories of Gyges and Croesus (Document 1) or Hermotimus and Panionius (Document 5). Other times, Herodotus says, tisis strikes even when a person has good intentions, as in the case of Croesus.

Tisis is part of Herodotus's complex presentation of the interaction of the supernatural and the human. He does not describe gods as intervening directly in individual human lives—that is, gods never tell an individual how to act, as they do in Homer's *Iliad* and *Odyssey*. But Herodotus does describe a divine effect on history on a larger scale by claiming that the gods supported the Greeks in their fight against the Persians. In one of his few direct comments on this narrative, Herodotus says that in defeating the Persian king and his army, it was the gods who held first place, followed closely by the Athenians in second.[8] Through his choice of stories, Herodotus sought to motivate his audience to think about how and why human power and fortune rise and fall.

---

[8]Ibid., bk. 7, sec. 139.

THE LIFE OF SIMA QIAN (CA. 145–CA. 86 BCE)

Most of what we know about the life of Sima Qian (Ssu-ma Ch'ien)[9] comes directly from his own writings (Document 7). He was born about 145 BCE near Longmen, China. By this time, the history of China stretched back nearly two thousand years, but it had been a unified empire only since 221 BCE, when the First Emperor of Qin (259–210 BCE) completed the conquest of China's formerly independent regions and established the Qin dynasty (see Map 2). The emperor made himself the first ruler of a government controlling all of China. The Qin dynasty lasted for less than twenty years, but the Han dynasty (206 BCE–220 CE) that replaced it kept China together politically for centuries.[10]

Since the frequent wars among pre-imperial China's different regions had often led to a defeated ruler being thrown from power, the emperors worried that opposition to their rule, however slight, might produce a rebellion. Emperors therefore reacted harshly to any hint of treachery or disloyalty. They especially feared that historians would write about past tyrannical rulers as a way to stimulate resistance to the present ruling family. In 213 BCE, the First Emperor of Qin ordered most books with any historical content burned in public and executed more than 460 scholars because he thought they were using stories about rulers from the past to criticize him and his policies (Document 8).

When Sima Qian was about five years old, his father, Sima Tan, became Grand Astrologer at the court of the Han dynasty emperor Wu (r. 141–87 BCE). His father's duties centered on keeping track of the movements of the planets and stars and linking these celestial events to things that happened on earth. The purpose of the records was to provide the emperor with clues to the meaning of anything that occurred in his land and to provide him with a calendar indicating

[9]Chinese is "romanized"—transliterated into Western alphabets—according to different systems, most notably Pinyin (used in this book) and Wade-Gilles, which can result in different spellings in English. The Library of Congress Pinyin Conversion Project discusses Chinese romanization and provides a conversion chart of the systems: www.loc.gov/catdir/pinyin/romcover.html. Sima (or Ssu-ma) is the historian's last (or family) name, which is given first, in accordance with Chinese usage.

[10]The rule of the Han dynasty is subdivided into two periods, the Former (or Western) Han (206 BCE–9 CE) and the Later (or Eastern) Han (25–220 CE), with the Xin dynasty ruling briefly in between.

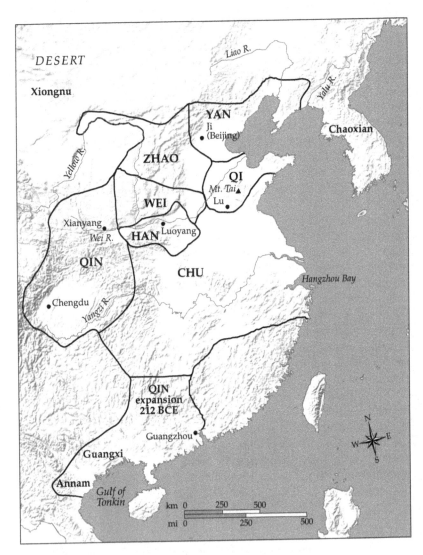

Map 2. *The Conquests of the Qin Dynasty, 221 BCE*

The king of Qin, a region in China, made himself the First Emperor of Qin by defeating the other regional states in China and unifying the country under imperial rule. Although his dynasty lasted only fifteen years, the emperor's unification of China changed the course of Chinese history, and the imperial dynasties that followed continued until the revolutions of the twentieth century.

lucky and unlucky days for performing political and religious cere-monies. The Grand Astrologer's job required studying the past, from astronomical patterns to works of philosophy and literature (which were the earliest sources for Chinese history), but the Grand Astrol-oger did not have the official duty of writing a narrative history. (It therefore seems misleading to translate the job title as "Grand Histo-rian," as is sometimes done.)[11]

Sima Qian received the extensive schooling appropriate for the son of an educated father working at court: He could recite ancient texts from memory by the time he was ten years old. When he was twenty, he traveled throughout China to visit famous sites and historical landmarks. Not long afterward, he obtained a job at the imperial court. Over the next decade, he evidently performed well because in 111 BCE, Emperor Wu sent him on an expedition to reorganize part of the emperor's territory. Sima Tan died in 110 BCE, and in 108 BCE the emperor promoted Sima Qian to the position of Grand Astrologer. Sima Qian worked as an imperial official for the rest of his life, but at great personal cost.

The turning point in Sima Qian's life, though he could not have grasped it at the time, came when his father lay dying. On his deathbed, Sima Tan asked his son to finish the work of history that he had begun. Writing this work had not been part of Sima Tan's official duties for the emperor. Rather, he began writing this history on his own because he strongly believed it was valuable as a guide to proper conduct in the present. He thought that private individuals and rulers alike could learn from history by imitating past examples of virtue and dignity and avoid-ing examples of cruelty and greed. This notion about the purpose of his-tory was widely accepted in Chinese civilization because of the writings of Confucius, a philosopher of the sixth century BCE (and therefore, incidentally, a century before Herodotus) and the most famous and con-troversial figure in Chinese history. Confucius is best known in the Western world for his work *Analects* (*Excerpts*), a collection of his say-ings and conversations, as well as events from his life.

Sima Qian reports that as a young man he studied Confucius and later used the *Analects* and other works attributed to Confucius as important historical sources and, above all, as a guide to the purpose

---

[11]It is difficult to translate official Chinese positions precisely into Western lan-guages. The Chinese term translated here as "Grand Astrologer" can also be translated as "Eminent Grand Astrologer," "Prefect Grand Astrologer," "Duke Grand Astrologer," or "Gentleman Grand Astrologer."

of his work. Confucius respected the past because he believed that people could best learn how to behave properly in China's hierarchical society by studying the great deeds of their ancestors and by immersing themselves in the customs handed down over the generations. Confucius insisted that history mattered above all because worthwhile new developments could only emerge from the cultural traditions of the past. For Confucius, the historian's job was simply to transmit knowledge of the past accurately without changing or interpreting it. This would guarantee the objectivity of the historian's account.

SIMA QIAN'S HISTORICAL WORK: *THE RECORDS OF THE HISTORIAN*

Sima Tan had intended to write a history of the world, which meant the history of China and the non-Chinese peoples on its borders, whom the Chinese looked down on as barbarians and culturally inferior. No one had ever written such a work before. Moreover, when Sima Qian promised to obey his father's wishes and complete this ambitious project, he was accepting a solemn duty, because obedience and loyalty to parents were central values of Chinese civilization. It is not certain how much Sima Tan had written before his death, but it seems clear that Sima Qian wrote most of this groundbreaking work, *The Records of the Historian*.[12] Like his father, Sima Qian worked on his history as a private project, not as part of his job. Still, his position as a high-ranking imperial official gave him access to court documents that allowed him to study valuable historical sources.

Sima Qian apparently thrived in the emperor's service until 99 BCE. At that point, he experienced the truth of the Chinese saying that "to serve the emperor" was "to wait for punishment." One of Sima Qian's acquaintances at court, Li Ling, had served Emperor Wu well as a successful general for years. In 99 BCE, however, General Li found himself in desperate trouble with the emperor because, in a failed attempt to escape disgrace at court after losing a battle, Li Ling had surrendered to the army of the barbarian people whom the Chinese called the Xiongnu (Document 7). Since Emperor Wu's greatest security problem was to protect China from attacks by the fierce and predatory Xiongnu (Document 14), he tolerated no failures regarding

---

[12]The Chinese title is *Shiji*, which has also been translated as *The Records of the Grand Historian* and *The Records of the Scribes*.

this dangerous enemy. He accused General Li of betraying him and condemned Li to death. Sima Qian spoke up to defend this general whom he respected, reminding the emperor of Li's loyal service and his value if he could be saved to fight again for the emperor. Sima Qian's words evidently enraged the emperor, who threw him in prison on a charge of "speaking evil of his emperor." It was expected that Sima Qian would either pay a large fine to be released or commit suicide. Since he lacked the money to buy his way out of punishment and no one volunteered to give him the money, he faced death as his penalty.

As Sima Qian later explained in a letter to a friend (Document 7), he could not kill himself, even though that would have been the only way to preserve his honor publicly. His deep feeling of commitment to his father compelled him to try to survive despite the shamefully high price he knew he would have to pay. To obtain the emperor's permission to live meant that Sima Qian would have to accept an alternative penalty—castration and the shame-filled existence he would lead as a man disgraced by his mutilation and inability to father any more children (he already had a daughter). In 98 BCE, Emperor Wu had Sima Qian castrated in the palace room called the "silkworm chamber," so named because it was kept dark and warm like the rooms housing the silkworms that helped make the emperor rich.

It is impossible to exaggerate the shame and disgrace that Sima Qian endured as a result of his decision to take this punishment so that he could continue to write his history. To have died on the orders of an unjust emperor would have been honorable; to live as a humiliated eunuch was hell on earth. In his words, he survived as "something left over from the knife and saw" (Document 7). Two years later, Emperor Wu, apparently satisfied with Sima Qian's permanent degradation, reinstated him to an imperial position, as palace secretary. For the remaining twelve years or so of his life, Sima Qian worked for the emperor who had mutilated him, accepting this degrading life so that he could finish his secret project to transmit a record of the past.

CHINESE HISTORY WRITING BEFORE SIMA QIAN

China's rulers had been employing officials in positions like that of Sima Tan for a thousand years or more. Though not employed specifically as historians, these officials nevertheless had a kind of indirect historical duty because they were required to record various kinds of information, especially the performance of religious sacrifices and the results of divinations (ceremonies seeking to identify the will of divine powers and sacred ancestors). Since China had consisted of separate regional states before the First Emperor's conquests in the late third century BCE, there was a great deal of raw material for history in the official records of the regions' diplomatic missions, wars, assassinations of rulers in struggles for power, political and religious actions taken by the rulers, and natural events such as floods, earthquakes, comets, and eclipses that might signify divine approval or disapproval of the rulers' actions. These records were in the form of chronologically arranged lists of short entries, not long narratives, and were linked to the official state calendar.

This kind of work eventually came to be called the *Spring and Autumn Annals*.[13] Chinese tradition attributed the original and most famous of these annals to the philosopher Confucius and regarded his edition as a model of how history should be used for moral guidance in politics and government. The annals believed to have been put together by Confucius record events under twelve rulers of the state of Lu during the period 722–481 BCE. Confucius's *Spring and Autumn Annals* are brief and consist mostly of a straightforward list of official meetings, sacrifices, battles, and deaths. They lack any overt judgment or interpretation on Confucius's part. Still, later Chinese historians believed that Confucius intended his work to express indirect praise and criticism of rulers through his choice of which events to include and which to omit, the order in which they were recorded, and the words used to describe them. As Dong Zhongshu (ca. 179–104 BCE), one of Sima Qian's teachers, explained,

Confucius composed the *Spring and Autumn Annals* to record events of the past to explain events of the future. Therefore, when something happens in the world, you should consult the *Spring and Autumn Annals* to discover which events it records that are similar, and then puzzle out the underlying significance of its subtleties and mysteries so that you will understand the meaning of the event you are studying. . . . If you do this, alterations in the celestial realm and on earth and events that affect the rulers will become perfectly clear, with nothing left uncertain.[14]

---

[13]"Spring and autumn" is an abbreviation for the four seasons of the year, indicating that the work would be arranged annually (hence the term "annals"). The commonly used title *Spring and Autumn Annals* refers, strictly speaking, to the original text when accompanied by later commentaries, as became usual.

[14]Ban Gu, *Han shu*, chap. 27. Cf. Michael Loewe, *Chinese Ideas of Life and Death: Faith, Myth, and Reason in the Han Period (202 BC–AD 220)* (London: Allen and Unwin, 1982), 86.

Dong Zhongshu was so focused on learning from history about what to expect in his own time that according to Sima Qian, he spent three years in his room studying Confucius's *Spring and Autumn Annals* with such intensity that he never even once glanced out at his garden.

The moral judgments in Confucius's *Spring and Autumn Annals* were therefore so subtle and indirect that sometimes the lessons seemed hard to identify. Still, Chinese scholars such as Sima Qian were convinced that Confucius had filled this concisely written historical record with effective moral messages. As the philosopher Mencius (372–ca. 289 BCE) put it, "Confucius completed the *Spring and Autumn Annals*, and disloyal officials and wicked sons became afraid."[15] Soon after the appearance of Confucius's *Spring and Autumn Annals*, commentators on it composed elaborate works to puzzle out the moral lessons embedded in it. They believed that if the true nature of Confucius's chronicle was understood, it would reveal the principles and conduct that a morally correct ruler must follow and the errors and crimes that he must avoid to create and govern a just state.

Other early texts accorded great respect by later Chinese historians were found in the *Classic of Documents*.[16] They reveal how highly Chinese civilization regarded history as a source of moral instruction. Confucius was believed to have edited the *Classic of Documents*, but, unlike the *Spring and Autumn Annals*, it records words instead of deeds—that is, speeches and advice reportedly given by rulers from the eleventh to the seventh century BCE. The documents all have a moral purpose, offering guidance on proper attitudes and behavior to those conducting political affairs.

THE FORM AND CONTENT OF SIMA QIAN'S HISTORICAL WORK

Sima Qian did extensive research for his history. As he explains, he carefully studied ancient annals, searched for historical and moral information in earlier works of poetry and philosophy (especially those written by and about Confucius), interviewed many people, and collected information from the places and landmarks he saw on his travels. He also took advantage of his access to official records kept at the

---

[15] Mencius 3B9.

[16] As with many works in Chinese, translations of the title of this book are not consistent. It is also known, for example, as the *Classic of Historical Documents* or *Book of Documents*.

imperial court for his research. He quoted, often in full, so many docu-ments, poems, philosophical excerpts, songs, letters, inscriptions, and other texts that his work amounts almost to an anthology of earlier Chinese thought and literature. This method respected the Confucian notion that history meant simply passing down the records of the past, not creating something new. In fact, Sima Qian claimed that he was only transmitting the past, and some scholars have taken him at his word, regarding him as little more than a scribe writing down and stitching together what he found in the earlier works of others. In this view, he was objective to the point of passivity. Others, however, see him as expressing subjective interpretations of history through his bold innovation in the structure of presenting his material and his subtle comments on the stories he relates.

Sima Qian was emphatic about the importance of women in Chi-nese history. Given the hierarchical nature of ancient Chinese society, the women who mattered most were members of the ruling families. He therefore includes detailed stories about influential women, such as Empress Lü. Her history raises questions not only about the tradi-tional restrictions on women's roles in society but also about whether women had the same desire for power and ability to rule that men did (Document 10).

Since his goal was to record the history of the world (that is, the world of China and its neighbors), Sima Qian had to cover an im-mense amount of time and space. The beginnings of Chinese history reached back two thousand years before his time, into the realm of what today would be considered myth. For Sima Qian and his audi-ence, however, these stories about legendary rulers and their families were the true ancient history of Chinese civilization. Sima Qian's fin-ished book amounts to well over half a million words, roughly three times longer than Herodotus's. It was originally written on thousands of bamboo strips that were tied up in bundles with silk cords, much like rolled-up window shades. A wagon was required to transport the entire work.

Five-Part Structure of the Narrative

Writing such a broad history presented problems concerning how to arrange large amounts of information. Should Sima Qian proceed chronologically, trying to fit everything into one story arranged from earlier to later events? This was how some previous Chinese historical works had been structured. Or should he tell the story region by region? This was how other earlier historical works, such as *The Narrative from the States* and *Intrigues of the Warring States*, were organized. Both of these structures would require the narrative to jump around a great deal in time and space, as in Herodotus's work. Another option was to arrange the material according to themes or topics, such as politics, economy, and religion, as modern historians often do in writing world history.

Sima Qian invented a new narrative structure combining all these methods that would influence how later Chinese historians presented their work. Instead of simply proceeding in chronological order or region by region, he divided his material into five parts—"Basic Annals," "Chronological Tables," "Treatises," "Hereditary Houses," and "Biographies"—each of which was subdivided into chapters. The entire work totaled 130 chapters. (In modern editions, the letter to Ren An [Document 7] is often added at the end.) The five sections present different information about the same people, events, and regions (although sometimes this information is repeated in more than one section). In "Basic Annals," for example, the emphasis is on the events of particular time periods, while in "Biographies" additional information about the personalities and actions of significant people who lived during those time periods is presented.

Since Chinese tradition taught that form carries meaning, the details of Sima Qian's new arrangement were deeply significant. By dividing his history into overlapping parts and offering different perspectives on the same events and people, Sima Qian represents the multilevel structure of the world as human beings experience it and the open-ended nature of human perceptions about the world.[17] As such, the structure of Sima Qian's history implicitly expresses his interpretations of the past, stressing the complicated and overlapping layers of meaning that had to be teased out of a great mass of sometimes confusing or contradictory information. This innovation set his work apart from all previous history writing in China.

It is not easy to translate accurately into English the titles of the five sections of Sima Qian's work, an indication of the complexity of his approach to history. The first title is usually translated as "Basic Annals" (Documents 8–10). Subdivided into twelve chapters, this opening section narrates the reigns of the ruling emperors and empresses from legendary times down through the Qin and early Han dynasties.

---

[17]For a full discussion of this idea, see Grant Hardy, *Worlds of Bronze and Bamboo: Sima Qian's Conquest of History* (New York: Columbia University Press, 1999).

Since this overview provides the general context for all of Chinese history, it is appropriate to have it begin the work.

The second section is "Chronological Tables" or "Chronological Charts." Its ten chapters have short introductions followed by tables in grid form that relate events in different regions and reigns to chronological headings. These tables have complex graphic designs that change at crucial points to accommodate the intricate spatial and chronological information that Sima Qian is interrelating (see Figure 1). The tables allow readers to scan in one direction to see what the developments in a single state were over time, while reading in the other direction reveals the events that took place each year in the different states until the unification of the country by the First Emperor of Qin in 221 BCE. This section fittingly comes right after "Basic Annals" because it shows in concrete ways how time and space must be interrelated for history to make sense.

The third part of the book has the title "Treatises" or "Monographs." Its eight chapters are essays on topics ranging from the relationship of the gods and human beings to calendar reform, music and rituals, the management of rivers and canals, and the economy. They show that although history is full of both large-scale trends and major changes, all of these are caused by or have direct effects on individuals, especially those in power.

The title of the fourth section is "Hereditary Houses." Most of its thirty chapters tell the stories of important families that held official positions or received other benefits granted by the rulers that were inherited by subsequent generations. These families were constantly involved in the struggles for power among the competing regions before the Qin dynasty unified China. In this section, Sima Qian illustrates the errors in character and conduct that led to the moral decay, loss of power, and eventual disappearance of most of these once dominant families. A few chapters in "Hereditary Houses" concern individuals instead of families. Chapter 47, for example, is the earliest biography of Confucius. It is possible that these unusual chapters appear in this section because the individuals described, like the longest-lived hereditary houses, had families and reputations that lasted until Sima Qian's time. What is certain is that Sima Qian wanted to stress the importance of Confucius's ideas as a guide to how people should live in the present time.

Sima Qian's final section is commonly known as "Biographies" (Documents 11–14). Its seventy chapters constitute about a third of the book and mainly record the lives of individuals whose memory

Excerpt from **The Table by Years of the Six States; Chronological Table 3**

[Year BCE]	[Year of Reign] Qin	Wei	Hann[b]	Zhao	Chu	Yan	Qi
222	25 Wang Pen attacked Yan, subjugating King Xi. He also attacked and captured King Jia of Dai.[a] In the fifth month, the whole world celebrated with a great feast.			6 Qin's general Wang Pen subjugated King Jia. Qin terminated Zhao.		33 Qin subjugated King Xi and seized Liaodong. Qin terminated Yan.	43
221	26 Wang Pen attacked Qi, subjugating King Jian. For the first time, the world was unified, and the King of Qin became the August Emperor.						44 Qin subjugated King Jian. Qin terminated Qi.
220	27 Renamed the Yellow River "Powerful Waters." Made twelve bronze statues. Renamed the people "black-headed ones." Standardized the world's writing. Divided the empire into twelve commanderies.						
219	28 Built Epang Palace. Went to Mount Heng. Constructed fast roads. The emperor went to Mount Langye and returned by way of South Commandery. Built Apex Temple. Granted thirty households an advance of one rank.						

a In 228 B.C.E, Qin had subjugated King Qian of Zhao and taken his territory, but his son, Prince Jia, fled to the small state of Dai and made himself king there.

b Hann's row is blank because the state was terminated in 230 B.C.E.

Source: Sima Qian, *Shiji* (Beijing: Zhonghua, 1959), 15.756–757.

Figure 1. *Chronological Table from Sima Qian's Records of the Historian*

This table offers a graphic representation of political and military events as highlighted by Sima Qian. It shows how the arrangement of the information changes from separate columns listing events in different states to a single row after the unification of the country by the First Emperor of Qin in 221 BCE.

Sima Qian wished to preserve. (In this goal, he resembles Herodotus.) These chapters describe both individuals and types of people, such as authors of handbooks on war (Document 12), assassins and retainers (Document 13), and barbarians (Document 14). He tells these biographical stories with passion and detail, emphasizing information that illustrates individuals' moral strengths and weaknesses. He says that writing them was hard work, involving "doubt, danger, and choice," but was worth doing because he believed that the decisions and fates of individual people are the major factor in history. He also believed that personal stories have much to teach others about how to live properly. His work inspired the emphasis on biography found in later Chinese history and literature.

Like Herodotus, Sima Qian reports that divine power, frequently identified simply as "Heaven," has a role to play in history but does not directly control human fate. Like Herodotus, he gives the greatest weight to the actions of individuals as the causes of events, rather than to impersonal trends or interventionist gods. Therefore, he includes a great deal of dialogue and many speeches that reveal the intentions and will of human actors. His comment at the end of his chapter on Confucius is a hint to his audience about how they should think about the people he describes: "I try to imagine what sort of person he was."

One way to think about Sima Qian's arrangement of his material in different sections is to see all his sections as supplements to one another, similar in intention to the supplements that characterize Herodotus's work (which has no divisions that we can attribute to the historian himself). Unlike Herodotus, however, Sima Qian's process of supplementation is systematic, operating through interconnections between information presented in different parts of his book. His work's enormous length (and lack of an index) shows that he, like Herodotus, expected his audience to do a great deal of thinking on their own to make connections between related stories told in different sections. He believed that effort was important, because to study the past was, to use Sima Qian's metaphor, "to provide a mirror for oneself" that reflected what was good and what was not in one's character and actions.

Moral Judgments

Sima Qian, like Herodotus, expresses both direct and indirect moral judgments in his historical work. In the sections concerning early Chinese history, he frequently represents Grand Astrologers (the position he held) as giving moral advice to rulers and predicting disasters that would result if the rulers behaved improperly. He records, for example, that the Grand Astrologer Bo Yang served the evil King You of the Zhou dynasty.[18] Bo Yang warned the king that he was doing wrong by falling in love with Lady Si. He expressed this criticism by reading to the king historical records revealing that Si had been conceived when her mother mated with a lizard born from the spit of dragons of the Xia dynasty. (Like Herodotus, Sima Qian includes mythical stories and leaves open the question of whether they are important because they are true or only because people believe them.) Bo Yang expressed his moral stature as Grand Astrologer by predicting the fall of the Zhou dynasty due to the king's immoral conduct.

In seeing history writing as a means of uncovering and expressing moral judgments, Sima Qian was following a long-standing Chinese tradition. Since Chinese rulers and imperial officials were expected to use historical examples to justify their policies and actions, they were the primary audience for historical writing. It is, therefore, no accident that the moral judgments that Sima Qian expresses mainly concern the character and conduct of people in power. Sometimes he offers his judgments at the ends of chapters, while other times he simply quotes what others said about the moral lesson of a particular story. Sometimes he points his audience to a more subtle and complex form of moral judgment, especially when he reports a person's virtue and good conduct in one story and the same person's faults or crimes in another. Sima Qian evidently intended his audience to compare overlapping stories to make a meaningful analysis of a person's character and conduct.

Expressing moral judgments about the emperor was very dangerous in Sima Qian's situation. Given Emperor Wu's suspicious and vengeful nature, it would have been deadly for Sima Qian if the emperor saw himself portrayed in a negative way in *The Records of the Historian*. Could this be why Sima Qian's original chapters on his own time did not survive?[19] No one can say with certainty. Surely Sima Qian, remembering his model, Confucius, realized the potentially dangerous consequences of writing contemporary history with moral implications under the rule of a suspicious emperor ready to punish

---

[18]Sima Qian, *The Records of the Historian*, chap. 4.
[19]These chapters were already absent when Sima Qian's work was "discovered" in the Later Han dynasty. Later writers composed substitute chapters, which do not contain material critical of Emperor Wu.

for even a hint of criticism. Given the Chinese tradition that the past was a guide for correcting the errors of the present, Sima Qian's history of ancient events and rulers could be taken as criticism of the current emperor and his government. In any case, Sima Qian clearly states that he did not publicize his work or present the emperor with a copy of his book: "I shall store it on a famous mountain [not named here], to await those who will understand it and spread it throughout the countryside and all the capitals" (Document 7). Reportedly, Sima Qian's work only became known two generations later, when his grandson made it public.

Sima Qian had an enormous impact on later Chinese historical writing. Every one of the twenty-six dynasties of imperial China commissioned official histories following a simplified version of the structure pioneered by Sima Qian. These dynastic histories, called "standard histories," included basic annals, biographies, and sometimes treatises. They also had a moral purpose: They were meant to explain why the new dynasty was the proper and just successor to the fallen—and therefore necessarily corrupt—former dynasty and why the new rulers rightly enjoyed the Mandate of Heaven (divine approval of the regime). Unlike Sima Qian, the official historians who wrote these standard histories were following the emperor's orders and seeking his approval, so they could not afford to include controversial material about the contemporary regime.

CONCLUSION: COMPARING HERODOTUS AND SIMA QIAN

Comparing Herodotus and Sima Qian provides an opportunity to examine the patterns and purposes in the writing of history across cultures and across time. Identifying the ways in which their works are similar and different can help us formulate, though perhaps not definitively answer, questions about whether universal human behaviors and values exist cross-culturally and how and why regional differences emerge in human societies. The main question that the selections in this book are meant to illuminate is how and why Herodotus and Sima Qian made moral judgments and interpretations part of their histories and thereby made them part of their audiences' experience in thinking about the past.

At the time Herodotus finished his history, Greece had attained in less than a century levels of prosperity and cultural achievement unimaginable at the time of his birth. The development of coinage had made local and international trade possible at a greater level than ever before. Prosperous cities, especially Athens, spent lavishly on military forces to wage nearly constant wars against other Greeks, as well as on spectacular displays of their wealth, such as marble buildings and temples and elaborate festivals featuring parades, music, and drama. Like Croesus, Greeks in this period believed themselves to be "blessedly fortunate" (Document 1).

It is, therefore, striking to notice that Herodotus ended his book with stories of cruelty and revenge, capped by an anecdote that jumps back in time to Cyrus's founding of the Persian Empire (Document 6). The anecdote records Cyrus's remark to the Persians when they wanted to move away from their rough homeland to find a more prosperous life: "Soft men grow from soft countries." The Persians then decided to abandon the quest for wealth so that they would not "live as slaves to other people." It seems likely that Herodotus meant for the prosperous Greeks of his time to consider the examples of the cycles of success and failure experienced by states and individuals in the past. That required his audience to look for interconnections between various events described in his history and to form their own judgments about the individuals involved in those events. In this way, Herodotus might have hoped that his goal of ensuring that people remember and evaluate the past would be fulfilled.

Sima Qian also composed his history when his country had changed greatly in the course of about a century. The unification of China into an empire ruled by a single person led to centralized political authority and increased trade with and knowledge of peoples to the west, who had developed civilizations of their own. The Han dynasty emperors developed an imperial bureaucracy to handle trade, taxes, and other essential activities. They tried to ensure the loyalty of the bureaucrats by hiring them on the basis of merit and not whether they belonged to an elite family. The emperors made education in principles derived from the writings of Confucius the key requirement for obtaining an imperial position because it instilled respect for hierarchy and deference to authority. Under this system, the power of the emperor and his officials was absolute.

Sima Qian experienced the pain that this unlimited power could inflict on individuals judged to be disloyal. It seems reasonable to think that his history has so much to say about Confucius's ideas and individuals in power because those two themes were so important in his world. The Chinese believed that examples of behavior in the past provided the best models for living an upright life in the present. Therefore, writing a history describing such examples was one way to offer guidance both to all-powerful rulers and to those they ruled. These examples carried the moral authority bestowed by tradition in Sima Qian's world. Sima Qian gave his history a complicated structure because he recognized that the moral lessons it offered were not simple and he expected his audience to think hard to understand his interpretations. He also realized that because his culture regarded history as a powerful source of potential criticism of the present, he could not risk being seen as disloyal to the emperor. Therefore, he hid it away for later generations to discover.

What links the work of Herodotus and Sima Qian is their mutual goal that people would study their works about the past as guides to life, that they would see in history a mirror of their own moral strengths and weaknesses and be encouraged to live properly. Some historians today would accept this as a fitting goal for history writing; others would not. Either way, the issue for historians of every time and place remains for them to decide their role for themselves and state their goals clearly in the work they produce.

PART TWO

The Documents

Herodotus, *The Histories*[1]

1

How Asia and Europe Became Enemies: The Story of Croesus

This document presents Herodotus's preface to his work, followed by the stories of how Gyges became king of Lydia (in southwestern Turkey) about 680 BCE and how his descendant Croesus (r. 560–546 BCE) came to a tragic end. Notice the overall goals in writing history that Herodotus announces in the preface, especially his concern not just with Greeks but also with "barbarians" (non-Greeks). In the story of Gyges, Herodotus raises the issue of power relations between men and women, while Croesus's fall from power and fortune introduces themes that run throughout the work: the fallibility of human understanding of the world and the importance of tisis *(divine justice or retribution) in determining human fate. Scholars, beginning in antiquity, have asked why Herodotus would introduce Solon as the prototypical sage in Croesus's story, because most evidence suggests that Solon died before Croesus's reign.*

Preface: This is the presentation of the inquiry [*historie* in Greek] of Herodotus of Halicarnassus, which he presents so that what human beings have done will not fade through the passage of time and so that the great and amazing actions of the Greeks and the barbarians will

---

[1]The titles given to the documents in this section were composed by the author of this volume as convenient pointers to the contents of each selection. They are not part of the original text.

From Herodotus, *The Histories*, preface; bk. 1, secs. 5–13, 26, 29–46, 53, 71, 86–92.

not lose their fame, and in particular the reason why they went to war against one another.

1.5. . . . I am not going to discuss whether it happened this way or in some other way.[1] I will, however, identify the man whom I know to have been the first to begin unjust actions against the Greeks. Then I will proceed with my work, giving equal attention to small and large cities. For most of the cities that were great in ancient times have become small, and the ones that were great in my time were small before. Knowing that human happiness and prosperity never stay in the same place, I will discuss both equally.

6. Croesus, the son of Alyattes, was a Lydian who ruled all the peoples west of the Halys River [in central Turkey]. This waterway, which separates Syria from Paphlagonia, flows from south to north until it empties into the Black Sea. Croesus was the first barbarian to our knowledge who on the one hand conquered Greeks and made them pay him taxes, while on the other hand made alliances with other Greeks as friends. He conquered the Ionians, the Aeolians, and the Dorians in Asia, and he made a treaty with the Spartans. Before Croesus's reign, all Greeks were free. The Cimmerians' attack on Ionia, which took place before Croesus, was only a plundering raid, not a conquest of the cities.

7. Rule over Lydia, which had belonged to the family of the descendants of Hercules, passed to Croesus's family, the Mermnadae, in the following way. There was a certain Candaules,[2] whom the Greeks called Myrsilus, who ruled Sardis.[3] He was descended from Alcaeus, son of Hercules. . . .

8. This Candaules really loved his wife. In his love, he believed that she was by far the most beautiful woman of all. His belief had the following result. There was among his bodyguards a man whom he particularly liked, Gyges, the son of Dascylus. Candaules always discussed his most important decisions with Gyges, and in talking to him he also used to praise to the skies the way his wife looked. Things went along this way for a little while, until Candaules, who was fated for disaster, said something like the following to Gyges: "I see that you don't believe what I have told you about my wife's looks. So, since peo-

---

[1]He is referring to the story, not included in this document, of the journey of the young Greek woman Io from Europe to Asia and the conflicting reports about whether she was abducted or went willingly.

[2]A ruler of Lydia in the early seventh century BCE.

[3]The capital of Lydia.

ple put more trust in their eyes than their ears, figure out some way for you to see her naked." Gyges then burst out saying, "Master, what is this sick plan you are talking about, telling me to see her, who is my master, naked? A woman sheds her sense of shame when she takes off her clothes. People long ago discovered what is good, and we have to learn from them. One of those things is 'Everyone should mind his own business.' I believe that she is the most beautiful of all women, and I beg you not to ask for things that are not according to custom."

9. By saying such things Gyges tried to resist, fearing the bad that would come from this. Candaules replied, "Be brave, Gyges, and don't be afraid of me—I'm not testing you by saying what I did—and don't be afraid of my wife—no harm will come to you from her. I will plan it from the start so that she will not learn that you have seen her. I will position you behind the opened door in the room where we sleep. She will come after me to go to bed. There is a chair near the door, and she'll put her clothes on that while taking them off one after another. You will be able to look at her with no trouble at all. Then, when she walks from the chair to the bed, with her back turned to you, be careful that she doesn't see you and slip out the door."

10. Since Gyges could not get out of it, he agreed, and when bedtime came, Candaules led him into the bedroom. Candaules' wife soon arrived. Entering the room, she put her clothes on the chair, and Gyges looked at her. As she was moving toward the bed with her back to him, he slipped out—but she saw him leaving. Realizing what her husband had done, she did not scream and give away the shame that she felt, and she maintained the appearance of not having noticed—she was thinking about taking revenge on Candaules. For among the Lydians, and indeed among barbarians in general, it is extremely shameful even for a man to be seen naked.

11. For the time being she did not show that she knew and kept quiet. The very moment that the morning came, however, she explained things to the servants whom she saw were the most loyal to her and then summoned Gyges. He came when called, not suspecting that she knew what had happened—it was usual for him to come see her when she called. When Gyges arrived, the woman said this to him: "There are two ways open to you, Gyges, and I give you your choice of what you want to do. Either kill Candaules and have me and the kingdom of the Lydians, or you yourself have to die on the spot, so that in the future you will not see what you should not see, doing everything that Candaules tells you to do. It is necessary that either the man who made this plan dies or you die, you who saw me naked and did what custom does not allow." Gyges was at first so amazed at her words that he could not speak, but after a while he begged her not to compel him to make this kind of choice.

Finding that he could not persuade her and seeing that it was truly necessary either to kill his master or himself be killed by others, he chose to survive. So he asked her this: "Since you are compelling me to kill my master against my will, tell me, then, how are we going to attack him?" "Our attack," she answered, "will take place on the very spot where he showed me naked, and the assault will occur while he is sleeping."

12. Everything was prepared for the attack, and when night came— for Gyges had no way out, no escape, with her compelling him either to destroy himself or Candaules—he followed the woman into the bedroom. Giving him a knife, she concealed him behind the door. Once Candaules had gone to sleep, Gyges slipped out and killed him. He then had the woman and the royal rule, and Archilochus of Paros, who lived at the same time, wrote a satirical poem about it.

13. He held the royal rule, and a response from the oracle[4] at [the sanctuary of the god Apollo at] Delphi supported his rule. For the Lydians became enraged at what had happened to Candaules and seized their weapons, but Gyges' supporters and the rest of the Lydians made an agreement that if the oracle proclaimed that he should be king of the Lydians, then he would be king, but if not, he would give the rule back to the family of the descendants of Hercules. The oracle did proclaim in his favor, and so Gyges ruled as king. The Pythia priestess[5] did say, however, that the family of the descendants of Hercules would get their divine vengeance in the fifth generation of Gyges. The Lydians and their kings paid no attention to these words until they came true.

. . .

26. When Alyattes died, his son Croesus, thirty-five years old at the time, became king.

---

[4]"Oracle" can mean either the person giving the god's response to a question about the future or the actual words of the response. The responses were always in the form of riddling or puzzling statements that had to be interpreted and that could be wrongly understood by the recipient(s).
[5]The person who gave Apollo's response at Delphi.

[Croesus then conquered nearly all the peoples living west of the Halys River.]

29. When Croesus had added all these conquests to the Lydian Empire and Sardis was at the height of its prosperity, all the famous wise men of Greece alive at the time visited him, one after another. Above all among these sages came Solon the Athenian. He had made a code of laws for the Athenians at their request, and now he was sailing abroad for ten years on the excuse that he wanted to see the world, but in truth so that he would not be forced to repeal any of the laws that he had set up. For the Athenians were unable to do this on their own: they had sworn great sacred oaths that for ten years they would abide by the laws that he had set up.

30. This being the situation and having left home to see the world, Solon visited King Amasis in Egypt and in particular Croesus at Sardis. Croesus received him as his guest and gave him a room in the royal palace. Three or four days later, Croesus ordered his servants to bring Solon to his treasury and show him all the great and rich things there. . . . Croesus then asked him, "My Athenian guest, a long report has reached us concerning your wisdom and your extensive travels, and how your love of wisdom motivates you to see a large part of the world. A desire has come over me to ask who, of all the people you have seen, is the most blessedly fortunate?" He asked this because he expected to be the most blessedly fortunate human being of all. Solon, however, not flattering him and relying on the way things really were, said, "Tellus of Athens, my king." Amazed at this answer, Croesus demanded sharply, "And why do you judge Tellus to be the most blessedly fortunate?" To which Solon replied, "First, because his country flourished while he was alive, and he had sons who were both beautiful and good, and he lived to see children born to each of them, and these children all lived to grow up. And then, after a life spent in what our people look upon as comfort, his end was surpassingly glorious. In a battle between the Athenians and their neighbors near Eleusis, he came to the assistance of his countrymen, routed the enemy, and died the finest death. The Athenians buried him at public expense on the spot where he fell and paid him the highest honors."

31. After Solon in this way gave Croesus a warning by telling him about Tellus's many blessings, Croesus asked him who was second to Tellus, expecting that at any rate he would be thought to have the second place. "Cleobis and Biton," Solon answered. "They were from

Argos. They had enough money for their wants, and in addition they were very physically strong. Both alike won prizes in international athletic festivals, and this story is told about them. There was a great festival honoring the goddess Hera at Argos, and their mother needed to be transported there in a wagon. When the oxen to pull the wagon did not come home from the fields in time, the young men, afraid of arriving too late, put the yoke on their own necks and themselves pulled the wagon in which their mother rode. They pulled her for nearly six miles and stopped in front of the temple. The entire crowd of worshippers at the festival witnessed this deed of theirs, and then their lives came to a close in the best possible way. With them God demonstrated that it is better for a human being to die than to live. For the men of Argos standing around the wagon said what a blessed thing was the young men's enormous strength, and the Argive women said the same about the mother who had given birth to such children. Their mother, overjoyed at their deed and at the reputation it had won, standing right in front of the goddess's statue, asked her to grant to Cleobis and Biton, the sons who had so mightily honored her, the highest blessing that human beings can attain. When her prayer ended, they offered sacrifice and took part in the sacred feast. The two youths then fell asleep in the temple. They never again woke up, and in this way they met their end. The Argives set up statues of them in the sanctuary at Delphi, on the grounds that they were the best of men."

32. When Solon had thus assigned these youths the second place in happiness, Croesus broke in angrily, "My Athenian guest, are you discarding our happiness as nothing, making us no more worthy than ordinary men?" "Oh Croesus," replied the other, "you asked me a question about the human condition, when I know that divinity is completely jealous and prone to cause trouble. A long life lets a person see a lot and experience a lot that one would not choose. I think that seventy years is the limit of a human life. These seventy years amount to 25,200 days, if we don't count the extra months sometimes added to our [lunar] calendar. If we add an extra month to every other year, so that the calendar will synchronize with the seasons of the year, there will be thirty-five such extra months, which adds 1,050 days. The total of the days in the seventy years will therefore come to 26,250—and not a single one of them will produce events like the rest. Therefore, Croesus, human beings are completely subject to circumstance.

"You are clearly very rich and the king of many people. But as for the question that you asked me, I can give you no answer until I learn that you have ended your life well, since no one who is extremely rich is any more blessedly fortunate than the person who has just enough for his daily needs, unless he happens to be lucky and holds on to all his good things until ending his life well. For many of the wealthiest people have been unfortunate, and many whose means were moderate have had excellent luck. When a very rich man is unfortunate, he has only two advantages over one who has good luck; but the man of moderate means has many advantages over the unfortunate rich man. The wealthy man is more capable of fulfilling his desires and overcoming any unexpected disaster; the other has the following advantages. He is not equally capable of fulfilling his desires and overcoming disaster, but his good luck protects him in these respects, and he is uninjured, not sick, not experiencing bad times, has fine children, and is good-looking. If, in addition to all this, he ends his life well, he is truly the one whom you seek—the one who deserves to be called blessedly fortunate. Until his life ends, however, call him only lucky, not blessedly fortunate.

"Of course, it is impossible for anyone to enjoy all these things at once, just as no country can have within itself everything. Instead, a country will possess some things but lack others, and the best country is the one that contains the most. So, too, no human being is self-sufficient—he has one thing but lacks another. The person who unites the greatest number of advantages, keeps them to the day of his death, and then dies peaceably, that man alone, my king, can rightly have the name in question, in my judgment. It is necessary for us to look to the end of everything and how it turns out. God certainly gives blessed fortune to many—and then ruins them utterly."

33. Solon seriously upset Croesus by saying these things to him, and Croesus sent him away, thinking that he was of no importance. Solon seemed completely ignorant, since, disregarding present good, he advised looking to the end of everything.

34. After Solon had left, a great divine retaliation [*nemesis*] struck Croesus because, it seems likely, he considered himself the most blessedly fortunate of all. Right away he had a dream while asleep that accurately predicted the bad things that were going to happen concerning his son. Croesus had two sons, one disabled, being mute; the other was in every respect by far the most outstanding of his generation. His name was Atys. In Croesus's dream, this son died after being struck by an iron weapon. When Croesus woke up, he thought carefully about the dream, which greatly frightened him. He immediately made his son get married, and although in previous years the young man had served as a military commander of the Lydians in battle,

Croesus no longer allowed him to fight with the army. Croesus had all the spears, javelins, and weapons of war removed from the men's quarters and piled up in heaps in the women's living space; he was afraid that one of the weapons hanging on the wall might fall down and hit his son.

35. Now it happened that while Croesus was making arrangements for the wedding, there arrived in Sardis a man constrained by circumstance, who had blood on his hands. He was from Phrygia[6] and belonged to the family of the king. Presenting himself at the palace of Croesus, he begged to obtain a ritual purification from bloodguilt according to the local customs. Croesus allowed him to be ritually purified. The Lydians perform ritual purification very much like the Greeks. When Croesus had performed the customary rites, he asked him where he came from, saying, "Fellow, who are you, and what part of Phrygia did you run away from to take refuge at my fireside? And what man or what woman did you kill?" "Oh king," he replied, "I am the son of Gordias, son of Midas. I am named Adrastus.[7] The man I unintentionally killed was my own brother. For this my father expelled me from the land and stripped me of everything." Croesus answered, "You happen to be the child of men who are my friends, and you have come to friends. Here you will not go without anything, so long as you remain in my household. Bearing your circumstance as lightly as you can will do you the most good."

36. From then on Adrastus lived in the palace of the king. At this very same time, a giant hulk of a boar appeared on Mount Olympus in Mysia which frequently ventured out from the slopes of the mountain to ravage the grain fields of the Mysians. Many times the Mysians gathered together to hunt the boar, but instead of doing him any harm, they instead always came back with some loss to themselves. Finally, they sent messengers to Croesus, who said this: "Oh king, the biggest boar imaginable has appeared in our region and is destroying our work. We do our best to take him, but we can't do it. Now, therefore, we beg you to send us your son back with us, along with a troop of young men and dogs, so that we can drive it out of our land." This is what they asked, but Croesus remembered his dream and answered, "Don't mention my son again; I am not going to send him back with you. He is a newlywed and is fully occupied with that. I will, however, send back with you a troop of Lydians and all my huntsmen

[6]A region north of Lydia.
[7]This name can be translated as "Can't Escape."

and hounds. I will instruct those whom I send to use all their energy to help you in driving the beast out of your land."

37. The Mysians were satisfied with this answer, but the king's son heard what the Mysians had requested and rushed to see his father. When Croesus refused to let him go with the Mysians, Atys said to him, "Previously, my father, we thought it best and most noble for me to win glory by going to war and hunting, but now you are keeping me out of both, even though you've never seen me being a coward or a slacker. So what look in my eyes am I supposed to have when I go out in public? What will the citizens think of me? What will my newly-wed wife think of me? What sort of man will she think she is living with? You have to let me go on this hunt or persuade me with a reason why it's better for me not to."

38. Croesus answered as follows: "My son, it is not because I have seen any cowardice in you or anything else that has displeased me that I am keeping you back. No, it's because I saw a phantom in a dream while I was sleeping that warned me you didn't have long to live and were going to be killed by an iron spearhead. It was this apparition, then, that led me to hurry your wedding, and now it prevents me from sending you on this mission. So long as I am alive, I will use all my ability to steal you away from death. You are the one and only son I have. In fact, the other one, whose hearing is destroyed, I don't reckon as mine."

39. The young man answered as follows: "Oh father, it is understandable that you would keep watch over me, having seen such a dream. But if you're mistaken, if you're misunderstanding the dream, then it's right for me to explain that. Now the dream, you yourself said, predicted that I would be struck by an iron spear point. But what hands does a boar have to strike with? What iron spear does he brandish for you to fear? If the dream had said that I would die pierced by a tusk or something else like that, then you should do what you are doing. But in fact it was a spear point. Our battle here is not against men, so let me go."

40. "My son," said Croesus, "you win with this explanation of the meaning of the dream. Defeated by you, I am changing my mind and I am letting you go on the hunt."

41. Then the king sent for Adrastus, the Phrygian, and told him, "Adrastus, when you had been whipped down by unhappy circumstance—and I am not blaming you—I ritually purified you and took you in to live in my palace. I have taken care of all your living expenses. Now, therefore, you ought to pay back my valuable treatment of you by doing something valuable for me: Go with my son on this hunt and keep guard over him, in case any bandits should attack you during the trip and try to hurt you. And besides, you should go where you have the opportunity to win fame by your deeds. Your family has this tradition, and you, too, have strength."

42. Adrastus answered, "Oh king, under other conditions, I wouldn't go on this adventure. I think it is not fitting for a man in such a circumstance to accompany those of his peers who are doing well. To be honest, I have no heart for it, and there are many reasons holding me back. However, you are urging me to go; I am obliged to do what you want. I have to pay back the valuable things you have done for me. So I am ready to do this. As for your son, whom you tell me to guard, you can be certain that you will get him back, at least if a bodyguard's being careful means anything."

43. After Adrastus had given this reply, they set out, well supported by a band of young fighters and dogs. When they reached Mount Olympus, they started searching for the beast. When they found it, they stood around it in a circle and started throwing spears at it. Then the guest, the very one who had been ritually purified, the one called Adrastus, threw a spear at the boar and missed—but he hit Croesus's son. Struck by an iron spear point, he fulfilled the dream. Someone ran to tell Croesus the news, and reaching Sardis, he informed him of the combat and of his son's fate.

44. His son's death devastated Croesus, and especially when he considered that the very man whom he himself had ritually purified had killed him. He was in such deep grief at the circumstance that he shouted fiercely at the god of ritual purification to be his witness of what he had suffered at his guest's hands. He also called on the same god in his role as protector of the fireside and of friendship: as protector of the fireside because Croesus had given hospitality in his own home to the killer of his son, and as god of friendship because he had sent as his son's bodyguard the man who turned out to be his greatest enemy.

45. Next the Lydians arrived carrying the corpse, and the killer followed behind them. Standing in front of the body, he surrendered himself to Croesus, stretching out his hands and telling Croesus to have him executed over the corpse. He spoke of his previous circumstance and said that now, in addition to that, he had destroyed the one who had ritually purified him. He said he could no longer go on living. When Croesus heard his words, he felt pity for Adrastus despite his own situation. And so he said to him, "I have from you, my guest, complete retribution, since you have condemned yourself to death.

You are not the one responsible for this bad thing happening to me; you did it unintentionally. Some god is responsible, who long ago indicated to me what was going to happen."

Croesus now gave his son's body a fitting burial. When people had left the grave site, Adrastus, the son of Gordias and grandson of Midas, who had become the killer of his own brother and the destruction of the man who had ritually purified him, realizing that of all human beings he was the one burdened with the heaviest circumstance, killed himself on the tomb.

46. Croesus spent two years grieving for the son whom he had lost. At the end of this time, Croesus received a report that [the Persian] Cyrus, the son of Cambyses, had destroyed the empire of Astyages, the son of Cyaxares, and that the power of the Persians was growing. He began to think that if it was somehow possible, he should take down the Persians' growing power before they became great. With this purpose in mind, he immediately figured out a test for the oracles among the Greeks and the one in Libya [in North Africa]. So he sent messengers to various locations: to Delphi, to Abae in Phocis, to Dodona; others to the oracle of Amphiaraus and of Trophonius; and still others to Branchidae in Miletus. These were the Greek oracles that Croesus sent messengers to consult. He sent others to question the oracle of Ammon in Libya. He sent these messengers to test the oracles' knowledge so that if he found one that had knowledge of the truth, he could send a messenger to it a second time to ask if he should attack the Persians.

[Croesus instructs his messengers to ask the oracles what he would be doing one hundred days after they left. (He boiled together a tortoise and a lamb in a bronze pot.) The oracles of Apollo at Delphi and Amphiaraus at Oropos answered correctly. Croesus therefore sent them costly presents to win their favor.]

53. Croesus gave orders to the Lydians taking the gifts to the sanctuaries that they were to ask the oracles if he should attack the Persians and if he should make a treaty of friendship with another army. When the Lydians sent on the mission had arrived and presented the gifts, they put the questions to the oracles by saying, "Croesus, king of the Lydians and other peoples, believing that your oracles are the only true ones in the world, has presented you with these gifts worthy of your knowledge. He asks you if he should attack the Persians and if he should make another army his ally." This is what they asked, and the views of both oracles came to the same point: They predicted that Croesus, if he attacked the Persians, would bring down a great empire. They advised him to find out who were the most powerful of the Greeks and make them his friends.

. . .

71. . . . Since Croesus had made a mistake in interpreting the response of the oracle, he led his army into Cappadocia [in central Turkey], expecting to overthrow Cyrus and the power of the Persians. While Croesus was making the preparations for attacking the Persians, a certain Lydian, who was already well thought of for having wisdom, greatly increased his reputation among the Lydians for the advice he gave on this occasion; his name was Sandanis. He said, "Oh king, you are making preparations to attack men of the following kind: They wear pants made from leather, and indeed all their clothes are leather. They don't get to eat as much as they want but only as much as they have, since their land is so rough. And on top of that, they don't drink wine—they drink water. They don't have figs to eat or any other good thing. So if you win, what will you get from them, since they don't have anything? And there's this: If you are defeated, think how many good things you will lose. Once they've had a taste of our good things, they will hold tight, and they won't let go. For myself, I am thankful to the gods that they haven't put it into the minds of the Persians to attack the Lydians." In saying these things, he did not persuade Croesus. Before the Persians conquered the Lydians, they had no luxuries or good things.

[Croesus's attack fails, and Cyrus swiftly and successfully counterattacks Lydia before the Spartans can send soldiers to support their ally Croesus.]

86. In this way, the Persians captured Sardis and took Croesus prisoner. He had ruled for fourteen years, and the siege [of Sardis] had lasted for fourteen days. Just as the oracle had predicted, Croesus had put an end to a great empire—his own. The Persians who captured Croesus took him to Cyrus. He had heaped up a huge funeral pyre and had Croesus tied up and placed on top of it, along with fourteen Lydian boys.[8] He had in mind either to make a sacrifice to one of

---

[8]The coincidence between the number of years of rule and the number of days of the siege evidently, according to Herodotus, led the Persian king to see some divine hand in the outcome of events, which he commemorated by planning to sacrifice the same number of young captives.

the gods or to fulfill a sacred vow he had made. Hearing that Croesus was religious, he for this reason put him on the pyre, wanting to see if some divinity would rescue him from being burned alive. In any case, that is what he did. Despite being in such dire circumstances on top of the pyre, Croesus remembered that Solon had told him that no one among the living was blessedly fortunate. He concluded that Solon must have said that through a god's inspiration. When this idea came to him, he sighed and groaned. After a long silence, he said the name "Solon" three times. Cyrus heard him, and he told his translators to ask Croesus who it was that he was calling on. They went up to the pyre and asked him, but he remained silent until they forced him to speak. "Someone I would give a fortune for every ruler to talk to!" he said. Since this meant nothing to them, they asked him again. They kept at him, crowding around until he told them how in the first place Solon the Athenian had come to him and seeing all his great fortune, had shrugged it off as worthless, or something to that effect, and how everything had turned out for him just as Solon had said it would. Furthermore, what Solon had said concerned not just Croesus himself but all humanity, and especially those people who thought of themselves as blessedly fortunate.

While Croesus was telling this story, the pyre had been set on fire and was starting to burn all around him. Then Cyrus, hearing from the translators what Croesus had said, changed his mind. He realized that he, himself a human being, was throwing into the fire another human being while still alive, a human being who had enjoyed no less happiness than he had. In addition to this, he was afraid of divine vengeance and took into account that nothing in human life was secure. So he ordered the blazing fire to be extinguished as quickly as possible and Croesus and those with him to be brought down from the pyre. His men began to try but couldn't put out the fire.

87. At this point, the Lydians say, Croesus understood that Cyrus had changed his mind but that all his men were not going to be able to put out the fire. He then shouted out to the god Apollo by name, begging him, if Croesus had ever given him presents that he liked, to come and rescue him from his present terrible situation. As he called on the god with tears in his eyes, suddenly in a clear and calm sky, dark clouds gathered and a storm broke, with so much rain gushing down that the funeral pyre was extinguished.

In this way, Cyrus learned that Croesus enjoyed divine love and was a good man. Taking him down from the pyre, Cyrus asked him, "Croesus, who among human beings convinced you to attack my country and to make me your enemy instead of your friend?" Croesus then said, "Oh king, I did this—to your happiness and my own cursed bad luck. The god of the Greeks was responsible for this—he encouraged me to attack. No one is so mindless as to choose war before peace. In the latter, sons bury their fathers, but in the former, fathers bury their sons. It must have been what some divinity wanted, for this to happen."

88. This is what Croesus said. Cyrus took off his shackles and gave him a seat near to himself. He was very interested in him, and he and his attendants kept staring at him in wonder. Croesus kept silent, deep in thought. After a while, he turned and saw the Persians looting the city of the Lydians. He then said, "Oh king, should I tell you what I was just thinking, or should I stay silent for the present?" Cyrus ordered him to have the courage to tell him whatever he wanted. So Croesus asked him, "What is that large crowd doing so eagerly?" Cyrus said, "They are plundering your city and carrying off your property." Croesus replied, "They are not plundering my city or my property; I have nothing to do with those things anymore. They are making off with your property."

89. What Croesus said made an impression on Cyrus, who then sent away everybody else and asked Croesus what insight he had about the situation. Croesus said, "Since the gods have given me to you as a slave, I think it is right, if I have any special insight, to indicate it to you. Persians by nature are violent, and they are poor. So if you pay no attention to their plundering and acquiring a great deal of property, this is what you can expect from them: Whoever gets the most, you can look forward to him rebelling against you. Now do this if you like what I am saying: Place guards from your spearmen at all the gates to the city, and have them say to those who are carrying out property that they are taking it away to give an offering of a tenth of it to Zeus. You won't make them angry by taking away the property by force, and they will realize that you are doing right and will give it up willingly."

90. Cyrus was extremely pleased with what he heard, since it seemed to be an excellent proposal. He praised Croesus highly and ordered his spearmen to do what Croesus had proposed. Addressing Croesus, he then said, "Croesus, since as a man who was a king you are ready to perform valuable deeds and words, ask me for whatever gift you want right now." Croesus replied, "Oh master, you will make me especially happy if you let me contact the god of the Greeks, the god whom I honored most. I will send him these shackles, to ask if it is his custom to deceive those who treat him well." Cyrus asked what complaint lay behind this request. Then Croesus told him the story of his entire plan, the oracular answers, and especially the gifts he had sent, and how he had attacked the Persians after he had been encouraged by the oracle. While telling this, he came back again to his request to be allowed to complain to the god about it. Cyrus answered with a laugh, "You can have this from me, Croesus, and anything else you might need at any time."

When Croesus heard this, he sent some Lydians to Delphi, instructing them to lay his shackles down on the threshold of the temple and ask if the god was not ashamed for encouraging him with oracles to attack the Persians on the grounds that he would put an end to the power of Cyrus. Then they should show his shackles as the sort of offerings that came from that. This is what they had to ask, and whether it was the custom of the Greek gods to be ungrateful.

91. When the Lydians arrived in Delphi and said what Croesus had ordered them to say, the Pythian priestess, the story goes, gave this reply: "It is impossible to escape the fate that is destined, even for the gods. Croesus has paid the retribution for the offense committed by his ancestor of the fifth generation before, who, although he was a spearman for the family of the descendants of Hercules, followed the lead of a deceitful woman in murdering his master and taking over that position of status, which he did not deserve. Apollo tried to have the fall of Sardis take place during the time of Croesus's children instead of during Croesus's lifetime. The god could not, however, turn the Fates to a different course. He did, however, do all that the Fates allowed and treated Croesus with favor: He delayed the capture of Sardis for three years. So Croesus should know that his captivity came that number of years later than had been destined. And second, Apollo rescued Croesus when he was about to be burned up. As far as the oracle goes, Croesus is wrong to blame it. Loxian[9] Apollo told him that if he attacked the Persians, he would bring down a great empire. In response to that, he should have, if he was going to plan well, sent another messenger to the oracle to ask if it was talking about his own empire or Cyrus's. Since he hadn't understood what was said and didn't follow up, he ought to acknowledge that he himself was responsible for what happened. And finally, he did not understand the oracle that Loxian Apollo gave him about the mule. In fact, Cyrus was that mule. He had been born from parents of two different peoples, as his

[9]An epithet applied to Apollo that means "elliptic" or "crooked," either from the perceived path across the sky of the sun, of which Apollo was regarded as the god, or from the enigmatic nature of the responses from Apollo's oracle.

mother came from a people with higher status, his father from a lesser people. She was a Mede, the daughter of Astyages, king of the Medes; he was a Persian, ruled by Medes. Ranking below her in every way, he was married to her who was his master." This was the response that the Pythian priestess gave the Lydians, who brought it back to Sardis and reported it to Croesus. After he heard it, he realized that the fault with his own, not the god's.

92. This is the way it was with Croesus's empire and the first conquest of Ionia.

2

How Others Live: The Customs of the Persians, Egyptians, Massagetai, and Scythians

In these excerpts, we see examples of Herodotus's presentation of the customs of various non-Greeks, or "barbarians," from his own time of the fifth century BCE. The Persians, whose empire was centered in what is today Iran, are the most prominent barbarians in Herodotus's history, but the Egyptians also receive great attention, with all of book 2 devoted to them. Several themes relevant to the judgment of human behavior emerge from these passages about the customs of "others." Notice the information on the wide diversity in sincere religious beliefs, the importance of truth in human relationships, and the definition of masculinity.

1.131. The customs that I know the Persians follow are these. They have no images of the gods and no temples or altars; they consider the use of them a sign of foolishness. This comes, I think, from their not believing the gods to have the same nature as human beings, as the Greeks imagine. The Persians' practice is to climb to the tops of the highest mountains to offer sacrifices to Zeus,[1] the Greek name for

---

[1]Herodotus here uses the Greek name of the chief god of the universe, whom the Persians called Ahura Mazda.

From Herodotus, *The Histories*, bk. 1, secs. 131–38, 140, 215–16; bk. 2, secs. 35–37; bk. 4, secs. 46, 64.

the chief god of the universe. The Persians use this god's name to refer to the whole extent of the sky. They also sacrifice to the sun and moon, to the earth, to fire, to water, and to the winds. These are the only gods whose worship has been handed down to them from ancient times. At a later period, they began the worship of Urania, which they borrowed from the Arabians and Assyrians. Mylitta is the name by which the Assyrians know this same goddess, whom the Arabians call Alitta and the Persians Mitra.

1.132. The Persians offer sacrifice to these gods in the following way: They do not construct an altar, light a fire, or pour a libation, and there is no flute music, no wearing of garlands, and no consecrated barley cake. The person who wishes to sacrifice brings the victim to a spot of ground that is pure from ritual pollution and there calls upon the name of the god for whom the sacrifice is meant. It is usual to have one's turban encircled with a wreath, most commonly of myrtle. The sacrificer is not allowed to pray for blessings on himself alone, but he prays for the welfare of the king and of the whole Persian people, among whom he is necessarily included. He cuts the victim in pieces, and having boiled the meat, he lays it out on the softest grass that he can find, clover in particular. When everything is ready, one of the mages[2] comes forward and chants a hymn, which they say describes the origin of the gods. It is not lawful to offer a sacrifice unless there is a mage present. After waiting a short time, the sacrificer carries the meat of the victim away with him to use as he likes.

1.133. Of all the days in the year, the one they celebrate the most is their birthday. It is customary to serve much more food on that day than usual. The richer Persians have an ox, a horse, a camel, and an ass roasted whole for the meal; poorer people cook smaller kinds of cattle. They eat relatively few main courses but many extra courses, which they serve a few dishes at a time. For this reason, the Persians say that the Greeks leave a meal hungry because they have nothing worth mentioning served to them as an extra after the meats and that if the Greeks did have extra courses served, they would never stop eating. The Persians love wine and drink large amounts of it. It is forbidden to vomit or urinate in front of another person. They have to be careful about these behaviors, but it is their custom to be drunk when they are deciding important matters. Then on the next day, when they are sober, the master of the house in which they made the decision puts it before them again. If they come to the same decision, they act

---

[2]Holy wise men.

on it; if not, they set it aside. Sometimes, however, they are sober at their first session, but in this case they always reconsider the matter while drunk.

1.134. When they meet another person in the street, you can tell if the people meeting are of equal status by the following indication: If they are, instead of speaking, they kiss each other on the lips. In the case where one is a little inferior to the other, the kiss is given on the cheek. Where the difference of rank is great, the inferior lies down on the ground in front of the superior. Concerning other peoples, they give the highest respect to those living closest to them, whom they honor second to themselves. They pay the next-highest honor to peoples who live beyond these, and so on with the rest. The farther away other peoples live, the less the Persians respect them. The reason is that they regard themselves as very greatly superior in all respects to the rest of humanity, believing that other peoples' excellence is directly proportional to how close they live to Persia. Therefore, they think that those who live the greatest distance from them must be the worst. When the Medes[3] ruled Persia, the various peoples in the empire exercised authority over each other in this order: The Medes were masters over everyone else and governed the peoples on the borders. These peoples in turn governed the peoples beyond, who in similar fashion dominated the peoples on their borders. And this is the order that the Persians also follow in their distribution of respect. Like the Medes, they employ a hierarchy of rank in administration and government.

1.135. No one so readily adopts foreign customs as the Persians. For this reason, they wear clothing like that of the Medes, considering it superior to their own. In war, they wear Egyptian armor to protect their chests. As soon as they hear of any luxury from any country, they instantly make it their own. In particular, they learned from the Greeks to have sex with adolescent boys. Each man has several wives and an even greater number of concubines.

1.136. In terms of manliness, manly courage on the battlefield is the greatest proof, with fathering many sons the second greatest. Every year the king sends rich gifts to the man who has produced the largest number: They believe that large quantity is strength. They carefully educate their sons from the age of five to the age of twenty in only three subjects: riding horses, shooting arrows, and speaking the truth. Until boys are five, they are not allowed to come into the sight of their fathers, but instead spend their time with the women. They do

---

[3]The original inhabitants of central Iran.

this so that if the child dies young, the father will not be saddened at losing him.

1.137. I praise this custom, and the following one, too: The king does not put anyone to death for a single instance of wrongdoing, and no Persian inflicts an extreme penalty on a slave for a single instance of wrongdoing. In every case, the previous services of the offender must be weighed against his crimes. The person suffering harm can punish the wrongdoer only if the latter's bad deeds outweigh the good.

The Persians insist no one among them has ever killed his own father or mother. They are sure that in every such case, if a thorough investigation were conducted, it would be discovered that the child involved was either substituted at birth [for the biological child] or else was the offspring of adultery. It is highly unlikely, they say, that a child would kill its biological father.

1.138. They believe that it is not permitted to talk about anything they are forbidden to do. The most disgraceful thing in the world, they think, is to tell a lie. The next worst is to owe a debt because, among other reasons, the debtor by necessity must tell lies. If a Persian city resident has leprosy or a skin disease with white scabs, he is forbidden to enter the city or to have any dealings with other Persians. He must, they say, have sinned against the sun. They compel foreigners afflicted by this disease to leave the country, and they even drive off white pigeons on the grounds that they are guilty of the same crime. They never urinate or spit into a river, and they never wash their hands in one. They do not allow other people to do this either, because they have great respect for rivers.

. . .

1.140. I can say all these things about the Persians with complete certainty, relying on my own personal knowledge. It is reported, however, that they have other customs concerning corpses about which they speak only indirectly, as if it is secret knowledge. The body of a male Persian is not buried until a dog or a bird of prey has mutilated it. There is no doubt that the mages do this, because they do it openly. They coat the dead bodies with wax and then bury them in the earth. The mages are very different from the rest of humankind and not at all like priests in Egypt. For religious reasons, Egyptian priests do not kill any live animals except those offered in sacrifice. The mages, on the other hand, kill animals of all kinds with their own hands, except for dogs and human beings. They even seem to enjoy doing this, and they make it into a big competition by killing without discrimination ants, snakes, and indeed any creature that crawls or flies. Since this has been their custom from the beginning, let them keep it. I now return to the story that I was telling before.

. . .

1.215. The Massagetai are similar to the Scythians in their clothing and their overall way of life.[4] They fight both as infantry and cavalry with bows and spears, but the battle-ax is their principal weapon. All their combat equipment is made from gold and bronze. . . .

1.216. Their customs are these. Each man marries one woman, but the men share the woman in common. Some Greeks say that this is what the Scythians do, but in fact it is the Massagetai. . . . If a Massagetai man wants a certain woman, he hangs his quiver at the front of her wagon. They then have sex without worry. The only boundary to life is this: When someone becomes old, all his relatives get together and sacrifice him with some sheep. They then cook all the meat and have a banquet. They believe this to be the most blessedly fortunate thing. If someone dies from disease, they bury him instead of eating him, regarding it as a misfortune that he did not get to be sacrificed. They do not plant crops, instead living on herded animals and fish; they find plentiful fish in the Araxes River. They drink milk. Of the gods, they worship only the sun, sacrificing horses to it. Their idea is that the fastest of all the gods should receive distributions of the fastest living creatures.

. . .

2.35. Concerning Egypt itself I am going to say a great deal because there is no country that possesses so many amazing things or has such a large number of buildings and monuments that defy description. Not only is the climate different from that of the rest of the world and the rivers unlike any other rivers, but the people also, in the majority of their ways and customs, exactly reverse what the rest of humanity usually does. The women there participate in the markets and in trade, while the men sit at home weaving on a loom. And while the rest of the world works the woof up the warp while weaving, the Egyptians work it down. The women also carry loads on their shoulders, while the men carry them on their heads. They eat their food

[4]Both were Asian nomadic peoples living north of the Black Sea and in the Caucasus region.

out-of-doors in the streets, but they withdraw into their houses to go to the bathroom, explaining that what is shameful but necessary should be done in private, but that which has nothing shameful about it should be done openly. A woman cannot serve as a priest, either for a god or a goddess, but men are priests for both. Sons are not required to support their parents unless they choose to do so, but daughters must, whether they want to or not.

2.36. In other countries, the priests have long hair, but in Egypt their heads are shaved. In other lands, it is customary for close relatives while mourning their dead to cut their hair short. The Egyptians, who shave their hair the rest of the time, let their beards and the hair on their heads grow long when a relative dies. All other people live their lives separate from animals, but the Egyptians always have animals living with them. Others make barley and wheat their food; it is a disgrace to do so in Egypt, where the grain they live on is spelt, which some call *zea*. They knead dough with their feet, but they mix clay, and even pick up dung, with their hands. They are the only people in the world, except for those who learned it from them, to use circumcision. Their men wear two pieces of clothing apiece, their women only one. They put on the rings and fasten the ropes to sails inboard, while others do it outboard. When they write or do math, they move their hand from right to left, instead of writing from left to right, like the Greeks. They insist that their method is "right-handed" and therefore dexterous, but that the Greeks' method is "left-handed" and awkward. They have two quite different kinds of writing, one of which is called sacred, the other "of the people."

2.37. They are excessively religious, far beyond any other peoples, and use the following ceremonies. They drink out of bronze cups, which they clean every day; there is no exception to this practice. They wear linen clothes, which they are especially careful to have always freshly washed. They practice circumcision for the sake of cleanliness, considering it better to be clean than attractive.

. . .

4.46. . . . The Scythians are the wisest of all peoples because they discovered the most significant thing we know about human affairs, but I do not like the rest of what they do. The greatest thing they found out is how to prevent the escape of anyone who attacks them and how to keep from being found if they do not want to be. Rather than building settlements or walls, as archers on horseback they all carry their dwellings with them, living not from farming but from their herds. Since their houses are on wagons, how could they not be invincible, or even impossible to meet in battle?

. . .

4.64. These are their customs in war. When a Scythian kills his first enemy, he drinks some of his blood and brings the heads of all those he killed back to the king. If he bring backs a head, he receives part of the booty. . . . He takes the skin off the head . . . and makes it into a hand rag, which he ties to his horse's bridle with pride. The man showing the most rags is praised as the best. Many Scythians use the skins to make cloaks to wear by sewing the scalps together.

3

Roping Asia to Europe: The Persian Invasion of Greece

In 480 BCE, the Persian king Xerxes (r. 486–465 BCE), the son of King Darius, invaded Greece to fulfill his father's sacred vow to punish the Greeks for what he believed was their treacherous defiance. He intended to make them Persian subjects, which to the Greeks meant a loss of the political freedom they cherished. To transport his huge army from what is today Turkey to Greece, Xerxes built a bridge across the Hellespont, the channel separating the continents of Asia and Europe. As Herodotus tells the story, note his attention to the themes of excess pride (hubris, or "hubris") and ambition, as well as the issue of cultural opposition rooted in geography (Asia/East vs. Europe/West).

27. Now there lived in Calaenae [in western Turkey] a certain Pythius, the son of Atys, a Lydian. This man entertained [the Persian king] Xerxes and his whole army in a most magnificent fashion, and he also offered to give Xerxes a sum of money for the war. Xerxes, at the mention of money, turned to the Persians standing by and asked

From Herodotus, *The Histories*, bk. 7, secs. 27–58.

them, "Who is this Pythius, and does he have enough wealth to make such an offer?" They answered, "This is the man, oh king, who gave your father, Darius, the golden tree, and likewise the golden vine. He is still the wealthiest man we know of in all the world, except for you."

28. This news amazed Xerxes, and now, himself speaking to Pythius, he asked him what the amount of his wealth really was. Pythius answered, "Oh king, I will not hide this information from you, nor pretend that I do not know how rich I am. Since I know that perfectly, I will make a full declaration before you. For when news spread about your expedition and I heard you were marching to Greek lands, I immediately had an accounting done of my money, because I wished to give you money for the war. The total was two thousand talents [nearly 114,000 pounds] of silver and 3,993,000 gold coins. All this I willingly give you as a gift. When it is gone, my slaves and my estates in land will be wealth enough for my wants."

29. This speech delighted Xerxes, who replied, "My Lydian friend, since I left Persia, no one but you has been willing to host my army, or to come forward of his own free will to offer me money for the war. You have done both, feasting my troops magnificently and now making the offer of a truly noble sum. This is what I will give you in return. You will be officially bound to me as a friend from this day, and I will supply myself the seven thousand gold coins that you need to have a round total of four million. Keep all that you have acquired so far, and always be sure to remain the same as you are now. If you will do this, you will never regret it for your whole life."

30. When Xerxes had spoken this way and had kept his promises to Pythius, he continued on his expedition. . . .

31. . . . He then reached Sardis, the capital of Lydia.

32. At Sardis, his first act was to send off heralds into Greece, whose mission was to demand earth and water [as symbols of submission], and to order that preparations be made everywhere to provide feasts for the king [and his army]. He did not send this demand to Athens and Sparta, but his messengers went everywhere else. He demanded earth and water from states that had already refused because he thought that, although they had refused when King Darius had made the demand, they would now be too frightened to turn him down. So he sent his heralds, wanting to know for certain how things would be.

33. Xerxes next prepared to advance to the town of Abydos [on the northwestern coast of Turkey], where his bridge from Asia to Europe across the Hellespont had just been completed. . . . Opposite Abydos, there is a rocky tongue of land that runs out for some distance into the sea. This is the place where not much later the Greeks under Xanthippus, the son of Ariphron, took Artayktes the Persian, who was at that time governor of the town of Sestos, and nailed him living to a plank. He was the Artayktes who brought women into the temple of Protesilaus at Elaeus and committed extremely unholy deeds.

34. The men whose job it was constructed a double bridge from Abydos extending to this tongue of land. The Phoenicians built one lane with cables of white flax, while the Egyptians used ropes made of papyrus for the other. It is not quite a mile across the strait from Abydos to the opposite coast. When the channel had been bridged successfully, it happened that a great storm arose and smashed the bridge to pieces, ruining all the work.

35. When Xerxes heard this, he became enraged and immediately ordered that the Hellespont should be whipped with three hundred lashes and that a set of shackles should be thrown into the water. In fact, I have even heard that he commanded his branders to take their branding irons and brand the Hellespont. It is certain that he ordered those whipping the waters to say, as they lashed the waves, these barbarian and reckless words: "You bitter water, your master is punishing you because you have wronged him for no reason and without experiencing any wrongdoing from him. Truly, King Xerxes will cross you, whether you are willing or not. It is right that no one should honor you with sacrifices, since you are truly a treacherous and sour river." While the sea was punished in this way by his orders, he also ordered the overseers of the project beheaded.

36. The men assigned to this duty executed the unpleasant job imposed upon them, and other master builders were put in charge of the work, which they accomplished in the way I will now describe. They tied together triremes and penteconters,[1] 360 to support the bridge on the side of the Black Sea and 314 on the other. They placed the ships at right angles to the sea and in the direction of the current of the Hellespont, in this way relieving the tension on the cables from the shore. Having joined the vessels, they immobilized them with unusually large anchors, so that the ships of the bridge pointing toward the Black Sea could stand up to the winds that blow from that direction and the ships of the side of the bridge facing the Aegean Sea could withstand the winds that howl from the south and southeast. A gap was left in the penteconters in no fewer than three places, to allow

---

[1]Two kinds of warships.

small boats to enter or leave the Black Sea as they pleased. When all this was done, they tightened the cables from the shore with wooden winches. This time, moreover, instead of using the two materials separately, they put six cables on each lane of the bridge, two of white flax and four of papyrus. Both cables were of the same size and quality, but the cables of flax were heavier, weighing nearly forty pounds a foot. When the bridge across the channel was completed in this way, trunks of trees were sawn into planks cut to the width of the bridge, and these were laid side by side on the taut cables and then fastened together on the top. This being done, brushwood was arranged atop the planks, and soil was piled up on the brushwood, then the whole mixture was tramped down into a solid mass. Finally, a fence was erected on either side of the lanes, high enough to prevent the mules and horses from seeing over it and being scared by the sight of the water.

37. And now when all the work was done—the two-lane bridge and the ship channel cutting through the peninsula of Athos, with its breakwaters about the mouths of the cut to keep the sea from sanding up the channel and its entrance—and when the news reached Xerxes that this last task was completely finished, then at last the army, after spending the winter at Sardis and now fully equipped, began its march toward Abydos at the beginning of spring. At the moment of its departure, the sun suddenly disappeared from the sky, even though there were no clouds in sight and the sky was clear and serene. Day was turned into night [by an eclipse], and Xerxes, when he saw this unusual event, was extremely upset and sent at once for the mages to ask them what this omen meant. They replied, "God is predicting to the Greeks the destruction of their cities; for the sun tells the future for them, and the moon for us." So Xerxes, hearing this, continued the expedition with a very glad heart.

38. The army had begun its march, when Pythius from Lydia, frightened at this sign from the sky and made confident by the king's gifts, came to Xerxes and said, "Grant me, my master, a favor that is to you a small thing but to me something huge, if you consent to it." Then Xerxes, who expected anything other than the request that Pythius in fact made, agreed to grant him whatever he wished and commanded him to express his wish freely. So Pythius, full of boldness, went on to say: "My lord, I have five sons, and it happens that all five are serving with your army in this march against Greece. I beg you to show mercy for my advanced age and let one of my sons, the eldest, remain behind, to be my support and the guardian of my wealth. Take with you the other four, and when you have accomplished all that you have in mind, come back safely."

39. Xerxes replied in a rage, "You wicked man, how dare you speak to me about your son, when I am myself on the march against Greece with my sons, brothers, relatives, and friends, you, who are my slave and duty bound to follow me with all your household, even your wife! Know that a man's emotional spirit resides in his ears, and when it hears good things, it immediately fills all his body with delight; but as soon as it hears the contrary, it swells with fury. Just as when you did good deeds and made generous offers to me, you were not able to boast of having outdone the king in generosity, so now when you have changed and become disrespectful, you will not receive everything that you deserve, but less. For yourself and four of your five sons, the hospitality that I enjoyed from you shall provide protection; but as for the one whom you value above the rest, you will forfeit his life as your punishment." Having thus spoken, Xerxes immediately commanded those to whom such tasks were assigned to find the eldest of Pythius's sons and after cutting his body in half, to place one piece on each side of the road so that the army could walk between them.

40. The king's orders were obeyed, and the army marched out between the two halves of the corpse. First of all went those carrying the baggage and the mules, followed by a vast crowd of soldiers of many nationalities lined up without any gaps, amounting to more than half the army. After these troops, an empty space was left, to make a separation between them and the king. In front of the king marched first a thousand cavalry of select Persians, then a thousand spearmen, who were also specially chosen troops and kept their spearheads pointing toward the ground. Next came ten of the sacred horses called Nisaean, all luxuriously harnessed. (These horses are called Nisaean because they come from the Nisaean plain, a vast flatland in Media that produces unusually large horses.) After the ten sacred horses came the holy chariot of Zeus, drawn by eight milk white horses, with the charioteer walking behind them holding the reins because no mortal is ever allowed to ride in the chariot. Next came Xerxes himself, riding in a chariot drawn by Nisaean horses, with his charioteer, Patiramphes, the son of Otanes, a Persian, standing by his side.

41. In this way, Xerxes rode out from Sardis, but when he felt like it, he would get down from his chariot and ride in a covered cart. Immediately behind the king there marched a troop of a thousand spearmen, the noblest and bravest of the Persians, holding their spears in the usual manner. Then came a thousand Persian cavalry of specially chosen men, then ten thousand, also picked out from the rest of the army and serving as infantry. Of these last, a thousand carried spears with pomegranates made of gold at the butt end instead of spikes. These troops were lined up surrounding the other nine thousand, whose spears had silver pomegranates. The spearmen who pointed their weapons toward the ground also had golden pomegranates, and the thousand Persians who followed close behind Xerxes had golden apples. Behind the ten thousand infantry came a body of Persian cavalry also numbering ten thousand, following whom there was again a gap for some 440 yards. Finally, the rest of the army followed in no particular order.

42. Xerxes' army [marched on northward], reaching the region around Troy. On this march, the Persians suffered some losses when they camped for the night at the foot of Mount Ida and a lightning storm struck them, killing no small number of soldiers.

43. On reaching the Scamander River, which was the first one of all those that they had crossed since leaving Sardis whose water was not enough and therefore failed to satisfy the thirst of his men and animals, Xerxes climbed up to the citadel of the [ancient Trojan king] Priam, because he had a longing to see it. When he had seen everything and asked about all the details, he made an offering of a thousand oxen to the goddess Athena of Troy, while the mages poured libations to the heroes who had died in the Trojan War. That night, a panic fell upon the encamped army, but in the morning they set off at dawn and . . . reached Abydos.

44. Once there, Xerxes wanted to view his whole army. Since there was a white marble throne located on a hill near the city that the residents of the town of Abydos had prepared ahead of time at the king's orders for his special use, Xerxes took his seat on it and, looking down from there onto the beach below, saw in one view all his land forces and all his ships. While doing this, he felt a desire to watch a race among his ships, which accordingly took place and was won by the Phoenicians of Sidon, much to the joy of Xerxes, who was delighted both with the race and with his army.

45. And now, as he looked and saw the whole Hellespont covered with the ships of his fleet, and the entire beach and plain at Abydos as full as possible of men, Xerxes congratulated himself on his good fortune. A short time later, however, he started crying.

46. Then Artabanus, the king's uncle, who at the beginning had spoken his mind so freely to the king and advised him not to lead his army against Greece, when he heard that Xerxes was in tears, went to him, and said, "How different, my king, is what you are now doing from what you were doing a little while ago! Then you congratulated yourself on your condition. Now you are crying."

"There came upon me," replied Xerxes, "a sudden feeling of pity, when I thought of the shortness of human life, and considered that from all this army, as large as it is, not one person will be alive a hundred years from now." "And yet there are sadder things in life than that," replied his uncle. "Short as our time is, there is nobody, whether it be here among our huge group or elsewhere, who is so fortunate as not to have felt the wish—I will not say once, but indeed many times— to be dead instead of alive. Disasters strike us, and illnesses make us miserable and troubled, making our lives, short though they are, seem long. Therefore death, from the wretchedness of life, is a very sweet refuge for human beings. And the god, who gives us the tastes that we enjoy of pleasant times, is seen, in this very gift, to be jealous."

47. "True," said Xerxes, "human life is exactly as you have described it, Artabanus. But for this very reason, let us turn our thoughts from it and not dwell on what is so sad, when pleasant things are before us. Tell me, rather, if the dream that we saw [that convinced us to make the expedition against Greece] had not appeared so plainly to you, would you still have had the same opinion as before and have continued to advise me against warring against Greece, or would you now think differently? Come now, tell me this honestly." "Oh king," replied the other, "may the dream that appeared to us come true as we both desire! For my own part, I am still full of fear and can barely control myself when I consider all our dangers, and especially when I see that the two most important things are both opposed to you."

48. "You strange man," said Xerxes in reply, "what, I ask you, are the two things that you mean? Does my land army seem to you too small, and do you think that the Greeks will have a larger force? Or is it our fleet that you think is weaker than theirs? Or are you fearful on both these points? If in your judgment we fall short in either respect, it would be easy to assemble another military force in short order."

49. "My king," said Artabanus, "it is impossible for anyone with any understanding to criticize the size of your army or fleet. The more you add to them, the more hostile will become those two things of which I spoke. Those two things are the land and the sea. In all the wide sea, there is not, I imagine, anywhere a harbor large enough to hold all your ships and provide them with protection if a storm blows in. And yet you need not one such harbor, but in fact many such harbors, one after another all along the coast by which you are going to make your advance. But there is not even one harbor of this size, and so we must remember that chance rules human beings; human beings do not rule chance. Such is the first of the two dangers. Now I will tell you about the second. The land will also be your enemy, because if no one resists your advance, as you march forward, being ever lured onward without realizing it (for who is ever satisfied with success?), you will find the land more and more hostile. I mean that even if nothing else stands in your way, nevertheless the distance itself, becoming greater and greater as time goes on, will at last lead to a fatal shortage of supplies. I think that it is best for human beings, when they take time to think, to be cautious and to consider all possible problems, but when the time for action comes, then they should act boldly."

50. To this Xerxes answered, "There is reason, Artabanus, in everything that you have said, but please, do not be afraid all the time, and do not dream up absolutely every risk that we face. If in everything that faces us you are going to focus on every possible problem, you will never achieve anything. It is far better always to have a brave heart and to endure one's share of bad things, rather than always to be afraid of what might happen so as to avoid ever meeting any trouble. In addition, if you are going to oppose everything that others say without yourself showing us the secure way that we ought to take, you are just as likely to lead us to fail as those are who give different advice. You are no different from them. And as for that secure way, how can you show it to us, when you are only a human being? I do not believe you can. Success for the most part comes to those who act boldly, not to those who consider the pros and cons of everything and are reluctant to try. You see how high the power of Persia now reaches. It never would have grown to this height if those who sat on the throne before me had thought like you, or even, if not like you, had listened to advisers with that sort of spirit. It was by brave actions that they extended their rule. Great accomplishments can be seized only with great risks. We follow, then, our predecessors' example in making this expedition. We started out at the best season of the year, and so, when we have brought Europe under our rule, we will return without suffering from lack of supplies or experiencing any other disaster. For one thing, we are bringing vast amounts of food with us, and for another, we will get the grain of all the lands and peoples that we attack, because we are invading a land not of herdsmen but of farmers."

51. Then Artabanus said, "If, my king, you are determined that we will not be in fear of anything, at least listen to the advice I want to offer, because when there is so much at stake, it is impossible not to have a lot to say. You know that [the earlier Persian king] Cyrus, the

son of Cambyses, conquered all the Greeks who speak the Ionian dialect of their language, except for the Athenians, and made them pay taxes to the Persians. Now my advice is that you on no account lead the Ionians against their fathers,[2] because we are certainly strong enough to defeat Athens without the support of the Ionians. Their choice, if we take them with us to the war, will be to show themselves either extremely unjust by helping to enslave the city that founded their communities or extremely just by joining in the struggle to keep it free. If the Ionians choose the side of injustice, they will do us only little good, while if they decide to act justly, they may greatly harm our army. Take to heart the old proverb, which expresses a truth: 'The ultimate end of an action is not always apparent at the beginning.'"

52. "Artabanus," answered Xerxes, "there is nothing in all that you have said that you are as wrong about as you are in saying that you suspect the Ionians' loyalty. Have they not given us the most secure proof of their allegiance to our cause, a proof that you yourself witnessed, as did everyone who fought with King Darius against the Scythians? When the Ionians had the full opportunity to save or to destroy the entire Persian army, they treated us honorably and with good faith and did us no harm at all. Besides, they will leave behind them in our country their wives, their children, and their properties; how could they possibly think of trying to rebel against me? Have no fear, therefore, on this score. Just keep a brave heart and support my household and my monarchy. To you, and you alone, do I entrust my rule."

53. After Xerxes had spoken and then sent Artabanus away to return to Susa,[3] he summoned before him all the most distinguished Persians. When they appeared, he addressed them in these words: "Persians, I have brought you together because I wanted to urge you to behave bravely and not to stain with disgrace the previous achievements of the Persian people, which are very great and famous. Rather let us one and all, on our own and together, exert ourselves to the maximum, since the action we are undertaking concerns the common good. Strain every nerve, then, I beg you, in this war. The men we are to march against are brave warriors, if what I have heard is true, and of a kind that if we conquer them, there is not a people in all the world that will dare thereafter to oppose our might. So now let us pray to the gods who watch over Persia and cross the Hellespont!"

[2] The Athenians.
[3] One of the Persian capitals.

54. The preparations for crossing the bridge continued all day. The next morning, the Persians burned all kinds of incense on the bridge and laid myrtle branches all along the way, while they waited anxiously for the sun, which they wanted to see as it rose. When the sun appeared, Xerxes took a golden goblet and poured from it a libation into the sea, praying, with his face turned to the sun, that no misfortune should strike him that would prevent his conquest of Europe before he had penetrated to its most distant boundaries. After he prayed, he threw the golden cup into the Hellespont, and with it a golden bowl and a Persian sword. . . . I cannot say for certain whether it was as an offering to the sun god that he threw these things into the water, or whether he was sorry for having whipped the Hellespont and thought that with his gifts he would make up for what he had done to the sea.

55. When Xerxes' offerings were made, the army began to cross. The infantry and the cavalry crossed over on one of the lanes of the bridge, the one toward the Black Sea, while the pack animals and camp followers crossed on the other, which was on the side of the Aegean Sea. First went the Ten Thousand Persians,[4] all wearing wreaths on their heads. After them came a mixed mass of soldiers from many peoples. These crossed on the first day. On the next day, the horsemen began the crossing, and with them went the soldiers who carried their spears with the point downward, wearing wreaths like the Ten Thousand. Then came the sacred horses and the sacred chariot, followed by Xerxes with his spearmen and the thousand cavalry, and then the rest of the army. At the same time, the ships sailed over to the opposite shore. According to another account that I have heard, however, the king crossed last.

56. As soon as Xerxes had reached the European side, he stood there to watch his soldiers as they crossed while being whipped [to make them walk faster and stay in line]. The crossing lasted for seven days and seven nights without rest or pause. It is said that here, after Xerxes had crossed, a man from the Hellespont region commented, "Why, oh Zeus, do you, taking on the appearance of a Persian man and the name of Xerxes instead of your own, lead the whole of humanity to destroy Greece? You could have done it without them!"

57. When the whole army had crossed and the troops were now on the march, a strange omen appeared to them, which the king ignored, even though its meaning was not difficult to guess. Now the omen was this: A horse gave birth to a rabbit. This showed plainly enough that

[4]The king's special bodyguards.

Xerxes would lead his army against Greece with great pomp and splendor but would have to run for his life in order to return home. There had also been another omen while Xerxes was still at Sardis: A mule gave birth to a baby that had both male and female genitals, with the former on top. This omen was also disregarded.

58. So Xerxes, thinking the omens unimportant, marched forward.

4   *Xerxes = Persians*

Death before Dishonor: The Battle of Thermopylae and the Story of the Three Hundred

When the Persian king Xerxes led his huge invasion force southward into Greece in 480 BCE, some Greeks submitted peacefully to him, but an alliance of thirty-one states decided to fight. A force of three hundred Spartans headed a small Greek force blocking Xerxes' advance at Thermopylae, the narrow pass through the mountains dividing northern from central Greece. Scholars still hotly debate why they did this: Was it meant to give the alliance time to gather its forces, or could it have been a suicide mission designed to inspire the allies to fight to the death for freedom? Or did the Spartans simply miscalculate the determination and intelligence of the enemy?

Herodotus frames this story with conversations between Xerxes and his Greek adviser Demaratus, a Spartan who had fled to the Persian court after losing a struggle for political leadership in his home city. His narrative raises the issues of the definition of true courage, what makes a man a hero, and how the Greeks' and the Persians' different political and cultural traditions affected their reasons for fighting.

202. The Greeks who at [Thermopylae] awaited the coming of Xerxes were the following: from Sparta, three hundred infantry; from the region of Arcadia, a thousand Tegeans and Mantineans, five hundred each; a hundred and twenty Orchomenians, from Orchomenus in Arcadia; and a thousand from other cities—from Corinth, four hundred men; from

From Herodotus, *The Histories,* bk. 7, secs. 202–15, 217–34.

Phlius, two hundred; and from Mycenae, eighty. Such was the number of men from the Peloponnese. There were also present, from the region of Boeotia, seven hundred Thespians and four hundred Thebans.

203. Besides these troops, the Locrians of Opus and the Phocians[1] had obeyed the call of their countrymen. The former sent all the troops they had, the latter a thousand men. The Greeks at Thermopylae had sent messengers to the Locrians and Phocians, to call on them for assistance, saying that they were themselves only the vanguard of the army, sent to precede the main body, which was expected to follow them any day now. The defense at sea was in good hands, manned by the Athenians, the Aeginetans,[2] and the rest of the fleet. There was no reason for them to be afraid. After all, the invader was not a god but a man, and there never had been, and never would be, a man who was not susceptible to misfortunes from the very day of his birth. And the greater a man, the greater his misfortunes would be. The attacker, therefore, being only a mortal, would of necessity have a fall from glory. With this encouragement, the Locrians and the Phocians had come with their troops to [Thermopylae].

204. The various Greek groups each had commanders of their own under whom they served, but the one to whom all especially looked up, and who had the command of the entire force, was a Spartan named Leonidas. . . . He had unexpectedly come to be one of Sparta's two kings.[3]

205. Leonidas had never thought that he would become one of Sparta's two kings because he had two elder brothers, Cleomenes and Dorieus. However, when Cleomenes died without a son and Dorieus also died, having perished in Sicily, the crown fell to Leonidas. . . . He had now come to Thermopylae, accompanied by the three hundred men whom the law assigned him and he had himself chosen from among the citizens of Sparta. All were fathers with living sons. On his way, he had picked up the troops from Thebes, whose number I have already mentioned, who were under the command of Leontiades, the son of Eurymachus. The reason he made a point of taking troops from Thebes, and Thebes only, was that the Thebans were strongly suspected of favoring the Persians. Leonidas therefore called on them to come with him to the war, wishing to see whether they would comply with his demand or openly refuse and reject the Greek alliance. They sent the men, though they did not want to.

---

[1] Both from central Greece.
[2] Greeks from an island just west of Athens.
[3] Sparta's chief military and religious officials.

206. The Spartans had sent men with Leonidas to Thermopylae ahead of their main army so that the sight of them might encourage the allies to fight and prevent them from going over to the Persians, as they probably would have done if they had seen that Sparta was slow to take the field. The Spartans intended, after they had celebrated the Carneian festival,[4] which was what now kept them at home, to leave a garrison in Sparta and hurry to join the advance force in full strength. The rest of the allies also intended to act similarly, because it happened that the Olympic Games fell exactly at this same time. None of them anticipated that the battle at Thermopylae would take place so soon. They were, therefore, satisfied with sending forward only an advance guard.

207. These were the intentions of the Greek allies, but when the Persian army approached the entrance of the pass, the Greek soldiers at Thermopylae were seized with fear, and they held a meeting to consider a retreat. The Peloponnesians generally agreed that the army should fall back to the Peloponnese and there guard the isthmus.[5] But Leonidas, who saw how upset the Phocians and Locrians [who lived nearby] became when they heard of this plan, spoke up for remaining where they were, while they sent messengers to the various cities to ask for help, since they were too small a force to make a stand against an army as large as that of the Persians.

208. While this debate was going on, Xerxes sent a scout on horseback to observe the Greeks, see how many they were, and check on what they were doing. He had heard, before he left Thessaly [just north of the pass], that a few men had gathered at this place and that at their head were certain Spartans under Leonidas, a descendant of Hercules. The horseman rode up to the camp and looked around, but he did not see the whole Greek force because he was unable to catch sight of those soldiers on the far [southern] side of the cross wall that the Greeks had repaired to block the narrow pass and now carefully guarded.[6] He did observe the Greek soldiers camped out in front of the wall. By chance, at this moment the Spartans were on guard duty outside the wall and so were seen by the scout. Some of them were working out, while others were combing their long hair. Seeing this, the spy was amazed. He counted the number of men, and when he had taken accurate note of everything, he rode back quietly.

---

[4]A month-long festival in honor of the god Apollo, during which the Spartans refrained from war for religious reasons.

[5]The narrow strip of land connecting the mainland to the Peloponnesian peninsula.

[6]There was an old wall at Thermopylae, fallen into disrepair, that earlier Greeks had constructed across the narrow pass to try to stop invaders coming from the north.

No one chased after him, nor paid any attention to his visit. So he returned and told Xerxes all that he had seen.

209. Hearing this, Xerxes had no way of knowing the truth—that the Spartans were preparing to do or die like men. Instead, he thought it was comical that they should be spending their time this way, and he called for Demaratus, the son of Ariston, who still remained with the Persian army. When he appeared, Xerxes told him all that he had heard and questioned him concerning the scout's report, since he was anxious to understand the meaning of the Spartans' behavior. Then Demaratus said, "I spoke to you, oh king, concerning these men long ago, when we had but just begun our march against Greece. You, however, only laughed at my words when I told you about all this, which I saw would happen. At all times I try hard to speak the truth to you, lord. Now listen to it once again. These men have come to fight with us for the pass, and it is for this that they are now getting ready. It is their custom, when they are about to risk their lives, to take care of their hair. Be assured, however, that if you can subdue the men who are here and the Spartans who remain in Sparta, there is no other people in the entire world that will try to raise a hand to fight you. You now have to deal with the leading kingdom in Greece and with its best men." Xerxes, who could not believe what Demaratus told him, then asked how it was possible for so small an army to resist his. "Oh king," Demaratus answered, "let me be treated as a liar if things do not take place as I say they will." But Xerxes was still not persuaded.

210. He allowed four entire days to go by, expecting that the Greeks would run away. When, however, he found on the fifth that they were not gone, and thinking that their firm stand was just insolence and recklessness, he grew angry and sent against them the Medes and Cissians, with orders to take them alive and bring them into his presence. Then the Medes rushed forward and charged the Greeks, but they fell in vast numbers. Others took the places of the slain and refused to be beaten off, although they suffered terrible losses. In this way, it became clear to everyone, and especially to the king, that although he had plenty of soldiers, he had only very few warriors. The struggle, however, continued during the whole day.

211. Then the Medes, having met so rough a reception, withdrew from the fight. The band of Persians commanded by [Xerxes' general] Hydarnes, whom the king called his Immortals, took their place. They, it was thought, would soon finish the attack. But when they joined battle with the Greeks, they had no more success than the Median squad. Things went much as before: With the two armies fighting in a narrow space and the barbarians using shorter spears than the Greeks, the attackers had no advantage from their greater numbers. The Spartans fought in a remarkable way and showed themselves far more skilled in battle than their adversaries. They often turned their backs and pretended that they were all running away, at which point the barbarians would rush after them with much noise and shouting. When they got near, the Spartans would whirl around and face their pursuers, in this way destroying huge numbers of the enemy. Some Spartans also fell in these encounters, but only a very few. At last the Persians, finding that all their efforts to gain the pass were of no use and that they had no success whether they attacked by divisions or in any other way, withdrew to their own camp.

212. During these assaults, it is said that Xerxes, who was watching the battle, three times leaped up from the throne on which he sat, in terror for his army. The combat resumed the next day, but with no better success on the part of the barbarians. The Greeks were so few that the barbarians hoped to find them unable to resist any longer because of their wounds, and so they attacked them again. But the Greeks were drawn up in detachments according to their cities and took turns bearing the brunt of the attack, except for the Phocians; they had been stationed on the mountain above the pass to guard the pathway around it. When the Persians found no difference between that day and the one before, they again withdrew to their camp.

213. Now, when the Persian king was at a loss and had no ideas about how to deal with the situation, [a Greek named] Ephialtes, the son of Eurydemus, a man from Malis, came to him and was admitted to a meeting. Motivated by the hope of receiving a rich reward from the king, Ephialtes had come to inform him about the pathway that led across the mountain above Thermopylae. By revealing this secret, he brought destruction on the band of Greeks who had there withstood the barbarians. Later Ephialtes, fearing the Spartans, fled into Thessaly. During his exile, in an assembly of the Amphictyons[7] held at Pylae, the delegates set a price on his head. After some time had passed, he returned from exile and went to Anticyra, where Athenades from Trachis[8] killed him. Athenades did not kill him for his treachery, but for another reason, which I will mention in a later part of my history. Nevertheless, the Spartans honored him. Thus then did Ephialtes perish a long time afterward.

[7]A regional alliance centered in Delphi.
[8]A region next to Thermopylae.

214. Besides this, there is another story told, which I do not at all believe, that Onetas, son of Phanagoras from Carystus, and Corydallus from Anticyra were the persons who told the king about the path and took the Persians across the mountain. One may guess which story is true from the fact that the delegates of the Greeks, who must have had the best means of discovering the truth, did not offer the reward for the heads of Onetas and Corydallus, but for that of Ephialtes of Trachis, and again from the flight of Ephialtes, which we know to have been on this account. Onetas, I grant, although he was not a Malian, might have known about the path if he had lived long in that part of the country, but as Ephialtes was the person who actually led the Persians round the mountain by the pathway, I leave his name on record as that of the man who did the deed.

215. Xerxes was now overjoyed. Since he approved highly of the deed that Ephialtes promised to accomplish, he immediately sent out Hydarnes and the Persians under his command. The troops left the camp about dusk. The pathway along which they went was first discovered by the Malians in this region, who soon afterward led the Thessalians by it to attack the Phocians, at the time when the Phocians fortified the pass with a wall and so protected themselves from invasion. Ever since, the Malians have always put the path to an evil use.

. . .

217. The Persians took this path and, crossing the Asopus River, continued their march through the whole of the night, having the mountains of Oeta on their right hand and those of Trachis on their left. At dawn, they found themselves close to the summit. Now the hill was guarded, as I have already said, by a thousand Phocian infantrymen, who were placed there to defend the pathway and at the same time to defend their own country. They had been given the guard of the mountain path, while the other Greeks defended the pass below, because they had volunteered for the service and had sworn to Leonidas that they would not yield their post.

218. The Phocians discovered that the Persians were approaching in the following way. During all the time that the Persians were making their way up the mountain pass, the Greeks remained unaware because the whole mountain was covered with groves of oak trees. It happened, however, that the air was very still and the leaves that the Persians stirred with their feet made, as it was likely they would, a loud rustling. At this, the Phocians jumped up and ran to get their weapons. In a moment, the barbarians came into sight and, seeing men taking up weapons, were greatly surprised because they had encountered the enemy when they expected no opposition. Hydarnes, alarmed at the sight and afraid that the Phocians might be Spartans, asked Ephialtes to which group these troops belonged. Ephialtes told him the exact truth, whereupon he put his Persians into battle formation. The Phocians, upset by the showers of arrows to which they were exposed and imagining themselves to be the special object of a Persian attack, fled hastily to the top of the mountain and there prepared to meet death. But the Persians with Ephialtes and Hydarnes ignored the Phocians and went on down the mountain with all possible speed.

219. The Greeks at Thermopylae received the first warning of the destruction that the dawn would bring them from the prophet Megistias, who read their fate in the entrails of the victims that he was sacrificing. After this, deserters came in, bringing news that the Persians were marching round over the mountain; it was still night when these men arrived. Last of all, the scouts came running down from the heights and brought the same news when dawn was just breaking. Then the Greeks held a meeting to consider what they should do. Opinions were divided: Some argued strongly against abandoning their position, while others argued the opposite. So when the meeting broke up, part of the troops departed and went home to their different states. Part, however, decided to remain and to stand by Leonidas to the last.

220. It is said that Leonidas himself sent away the troops that left because he was concerned for their safety, but he thought it would be shameful for either him or his Spartans to leave the post that they had been especially sent to guard. For my own part, I tend to think that Leonidas gave the order, sensing that the allies were losing heart and unwilling to confront the danger that he had made up his own mind to accept. He therefore commanded them to withdraw but said that he himself could not retreat with honor. He knew that if he stayed, glory awaited him and that Sparta would not lose its prosperity. For when the Spartans, at the very beginning of the war, had consulted the oracle at Delphi about the invasion, the answer they had received from the priestess of Apollo was that either Sparta must be overthrown by the barbarians or one of its kings must die. . . . The memory of this oracle, I think, and the wish to win the whole glory for the Spartans caused Leonidas to send the allies away. This is more likely than that they quarreled with him and took their departure in such unruly fashion.

Confused about this section?

221. To me it seems no small argument in favor of this view that the prophet who accompanied the army, Megistias from Acarnania[9]—said to have been of the blood of Melampus and the same one who had been led by the appearance of the victims' entrails to warn the Greeks of the danger that threatened them—also received orders from Leonidas to withdraw (as it is certain he did), so that he could escape the coming destruction. Megistias, however, though ordered to leave, refused and stayed with the army. He did have an only son present with the expedition, whom he now sent away.

222. When Leonidas ordered the allies to withdraw, they obeyed and immediately departed. Only the Thespians and the Thebans remained with the Spartans. Leonidas kept back the Thebans as hostages, very much against their will. The Thespians, on the contrary, stayed entirely of their own accord, refusing to retreat and declaring that they would not abandon Leonidas and his followers. So they remained with the Spartans—and died with them. Their leader was Demophilus, the son of Diadromes.

223. At sunrise, Xerxes poured libations, after which he waited until the time when a Greek marketplace is liable to fill and then began his advance. Ephialtes had instructed him on this, since the descent of the mountain was much quicker, and the distance much shorter, than was the way around the hills and the ascent. So the barbarians under Xerxes began to approach, and the Greeks under Leonidas, as they now marched out determined to die, advanced much farther than on previous days, until they reached the more open portion of the pass. Previously, they had held their position behind the wall and from there had gone forth to fight at the point where the pass was the narrowest. Now they joined battle beyond the narrows and slaughtered the barbarians, who fell in heaps. Behind them, the commanders of the Persian squadrons, armed with whips, urged their men forward with continual blows. Many were forced into the sea and perished. A still greater number were trampled to death by their own soldiers; no one paid attention to the dying. The Greeks, disregarding their own safety and desperate because they knew that, as the mountain had been crossed, their destruction was near at hand, fought against the barbarians with the most furious courage.

224. By this time, the spears of most of the Greek soldiers were broken, and they cut down the ranks of the Persians with their

[9]A region in western Greece.

Xerxes = Barbarian

swords. Here, in the middle of the struggle, Leonidas fell fighting bravely, together with many other famous Spartans, whose names I have taken care to learn on account of their great worthiness, as indeed I have the names of all the three hundred. Very many famous Persians also died, among them two sons of King Darius, Abrocomes and Hyperanthes, his children by Phratagune, the daughter of Artanes. Artanes was a brother of Darius, being a son of Hystaspes, the son of Arsames. When Artanes gave his daughter to the king, he also made Darius heir of all his property, as she was his only child.

225. Thus two brothers of Xerxes fought here and died. And now a fierce struggle arose between the Persians and the Spartans over the body of Leonidas, in which the Greeks four times drove back the enemy. At last, by their great bravery, they succeeded in carrying off the body. This combat was scarcely ended when the Persians with Ephialtes approached. The Greeks, informed that they were close, made a change in the manner of their fighting. Drawing back into the narrowest part of the pass and retreating even behind the wall blocking the way, they posted themselves upon a mound, where they stood all drawn up together in one close body, except the Thebans. The mound of which I am speaking is at the entrance of the pass, where the stone lion stands that was set up in honor of Leonidas. Here they defended themselves to the end, with those who still had swords using them, and the others fighting with their hands and teeth. Finally, the barbarians, some of whom had pulled down the wall and attacked them in front, while others had gone round and now encircled them upon every side, overwhelmed and buried the remaining Greeks beneath showers of missile weapons.

226. All the Spartans and Thespians behaved nobly, but nevertheless one man is said to have distinguished himself above all the rest: Dieneces the Spartan. People still remember remarks that he made before the battle. One of the men from Trachis told him, "So large is the number of the barbarians that when they shoot their arrows, their multitude will hide the sun." Dieneces, not at all frightened at these words and unconcerned about the Persians' numbers, answered, "Our Trachinian friend brings us excellent news. If the Persians darken the sun, we'll have our battle in the shade." Other sayings of his of the same kind are also on record.

227. After him, two brothers, Spartans, are said to have distinguished themselves. They were named Alpheus and Maro and were the sons of Orsiphantus. There was also a Thespian who gained greater glory than any of his countrymen: Dithyrambus, the son of Harmatidas.

228. The dead were buried where they fell, and in their honor, as well as in honor of those who died before Leonidas sent the allies away, an inscription was set up that said:

> Here did four thousand men from the Peloponnese
> Against three million bravely stand.

This was in honor of all. Another was for the Spartans alone:

> Go, stranger, and tell the Spartans
> That here we lie, obedient to their orders.

The prophet had the following:

> Here lies Megistias, who fell
> When the Medes came across Spercheius's[10] fords.
> Clearly, the wise prophet foresaw the coming death,
> Yet he scorned to abandon his Spartan companions.

These inscriptions and the pillars on which they were carved were all set up by the Amphictyons, except that in honor of Megistias, which was inscribed to him (on account of their sworn friendship) by Simonides, the son of Leoprepes.

229. Two Spartans from the three hundred, it is said, Aristodemus and Eurytus, having been attacked by a disease of the eyes, had received orders from Leonidas to leave the camp; both stayed at Alpeni during the worst stage of their illness. These two men might, had they been so minded, have agreed together to return alive to Sparta. Or if they did not want to return, they might have gone to the battlefield and fallen with their countrymen. But at this time, when either choice was open to them, unhappily they could not agree and took opposite courses. Eurytus no sooner heard that the Persians had come round the mountain than immediately he told his slave to bring his armor and, having buckled it on, ordered his slave to lead him [blind as he was] to the place where his friends were fighting. The slave did so and then turned and fled, but Eurytus plunged into the thick of the battle and was killed. Aristodemus, on the other hand, lacked courage and remained at Alpeni. It is my belief that if only Aristodemus had been sick and returned to Sparta, or if both had come

---

[10]A river near Thermopylae.

back together, the Spartans would have been satisfied and felt no anger. But when there were two men with the very same excuse, and one of them was scared for his life while the other freely gave it away, they had no course but to be very angry with the former.

230. This is the account that some give of the escape of Aristodemus. Others say that he, with another man, had been sent carrying a message from the army and, having it in his power to return in time for the battle, purposely wasted time on the road, and so survived his comrades, while his fellow messenger came back in time and fell in the battle.

231. When Aristodemus returned to Sparta, reproach and disgrace awaited him: disgrace, because no Spartan would give him a light to kindle the fire in his home[11] or so much as speak a word to him, and reproach, since all spoke of him as "the cowardly." However, he wiped away all his shame afterward at the Battle of Plataea [479 BCE].   *wow.*

232. Another of the three hundred is likewise said to have survived the battle, a man named Pantites, whom Leonidas had sent as a messenger to Thessaly. He, they say, on his return to Sparta, found himself in such disgrace that he hanged himself.

233. The Thebans under the command of Leontiades remained with the Greeks and fought against the barbarians only so long as necessity compelled them. No sooner did they see victory tilting to the Persians and the Greeks under Leonidas hurrying with all speed toward the mound, than they moved away from their companions. With hands upraised, they advanced toward the barbarians, shouting, as was indeed very true, that they for their part favored the Persians and had been among the first to give earth and water[12] to the king; force alone had brought them to Thermopylae. Therefore, they must not be blamed for the slaughter that had befallen the king's army. These words, the truth of which the Thessalians confirmed, were enough to obtain the Thebans the grant of their lives. However, their good fortune was not without some drawbacks. Some of them were slain by the barbarians on their first approach, and the rest, who were the greater number, had the royal mark branded upon their bodies by the command of Xerxes. Leontiades was the first to suffer. (This

---

[11]Refusing to help someone relight the fire that every house needed for warmth and for cooking was a sign of complete social rejection of that person.
[12]Symbols of obedience.

man's son, Eurymachus, was afterward slain by the Plataeans when he came with a band of four hundred Thebans and seized their city.)

234. In this way, the Greeks fought at Thermopylae. Xerxes, after the fight was over, called for Demaratus to question him and began as follows: "Demaratus, you are a worthy man; your speaking the truth proves it. Everything happened as you forewarned me. Now, then, tell me how many Spartans are there left, and of those left how many are as brave warriors as these? Or are they all alike?" "Oh king," replied the other, "the whole number of the Spartans is very large, and many are the cities that they inhabit. But I will tell you what you really want to learn. There is a town in Lacedaemon[13] called Sparta, which contains within it about eight thousand full-grown men. They are, one and all, equal to those who have fought here. The other Spartans are brave men, but not warriors equal to these."

[13]The Greek name of the region of Sparta.

5

Human Wisdom and Divine Vengeance: Artemisia's Advice and Hermotimus's Revenge

In 480 BCE, Xerxes burned Athens after the Athenians evacuated it rather than surrender. The Athenian commander Themistocles then tricked Xerxes into fighting a battle against the Greek fleet in the strait between the island of Salamis, just off the western coast of Athens, and the Athenian mainland, where the channel was too narrow for the much larger Persian fleet to use all its warships at once. The Greek alliance's victory in the Battle of Salamis turned the tide in the war and caused Xerxes to take his fleet back to Persia, leaving his infantry behind to fight—and lose—a final battle at Plataea, in central Greece, in 479 BCE. The Battle of Salamis therefore became a monument in the history of the ancient Greeks' defense of their political freedom from outside domination. In this part of his work, Herodotus, by foregrounding Artemisia, a woman commander in the Persian fleet, again raises the issue of what qualities

From Herodotus, *The Histories*, bk. 7, sec. 99; bk. 8, secs. 84, 86–88, 101–6.

might differentiate men and women, and whether there are any gender differences concerning courage in battle and quick thinking under pressure. He concludes the story with a "digression" about revenge. (See the discussion of Herodotus's "digressions" in part one.)

women in war

7.99. [Having listed Xerxes' primary commanders, Herodotus then says,] I am not going to give the names of Xerxes' other commanders because I do not have to, but I will mention Artemisia. It is amazing to me that she, a woman, took part in the invasion of Greece. She became the ruler of Caria[1] after her husband's death. Then, even though she had a son of military age and was under absolutely no compulsion to join the expedition herself, she nevertheless went to war, inspired by her personal will and manly bravery.... [The five warships she brought] had the best reputation in the whole fleet, after the ships of Sidon.[2] Of all the advice the king received from his allies, hers was the best.

Honor

. . .

8.84. The Greeks . . . now prepared themselves for a battle at sea [in the channel between the island of Salamis and the Athenian coast]. At first dawn, they held a meeting of all the men who were going to row the warships. Themistocles made the best speech of all. In short, his words compared all the things that were better to all those that were worse, everything that belonged to human nature and to disaster. At the end of his speech, he encouraged them to choose what was better. Then he told them to board their ships.

. . .

8.86. . . . The majority of the Persian ships were sunk or disabled in the battle at Salamis, with the Athenians destroying some and the Aeginetans destroying others. Since the Greeks went into battle with beautiful discipline and in order, while the barbarians were neither lined up nor did anything in the battle thoughtfully, it was predictable that what happened to the barbarians would happen. Still, on that day,

[1] A region in southwestern Anatolia (today Turkey).
[2] A city on the coast of Lebanon.
[3] An island off the eastern coast of Athens.

the Persians showed themselves to be far better than they had in the previous battle off the island of Euboea.[3] Every one of them fought energetically and with fearful thoughts of Xerxes, since it seemed to each one that the king was looking at him.

8.87. I [Herodotus] am not able to say for certain what part the various groups, whether Greek or barbarian, took in the battle. Artemisia, however, I know distinguished herself in such a way that gained her even greater respect than before in the eyes of the king. Once confusion had spread throughout the whole Persian fleet in the battle, an Athenian warship was closely pursuing her ship. She had no way to get away, since in front of her were a number of ships from her side and she was nearest of all the Persians to the enemy line. So she devised a maneuver that ensured her safety. Under pressure by the Athenian ship, she advanced straight against one of the ships of her own side, a warship from Calynda,[4] which had Damasithymus, the Calyndian king, himself on board. I cannot say whether she had had any quarrel with the man while the fleet had been in the Hellespont, nor can I decide whether she attacked his ship on purpose, or whether it was purely by chance that the Calyndian ship came in her way, but it is certain that she rammed his ship and swamped it. In this way, she had the good fortune to acquire two advantages for herself. First, the commander of the Athenian ship, when he saw her attack one of the enemy's fleet, thought immediately that her ship was Greek, or else had deserted from the Persians and was now fighting on the Greek side. He therefore gave up the chase and turned away to attack others.

Courage / wisdom

8.88. Thus, in the first place, she saved her life by this action and was able to get away safely. And second, in the very act of doing the king an injury [by destroying one of his ships], she raised herself to a greater height than ever in his esteem. For as Xerxes watched the fight, he remarked (it is said) on the destruction of the warship, whereupon those around him said, "Do you see, master, how well Artemisia fights, and how she has just sunk a ship of the enemy?" Then Xerxes asked if it were really Artemisia's doing, and they answered, "Certainly, for we recognize her flag." They all insisted that the sunken ship belonged to the Greek side. Everything, it is said, conspired to bring the queen good luck. It was especially fortunate for her that not one of those on board the Calyndian ship survived to become her accuser.

---

[4] A city in southwestern Turkey.

female commander

Xerxes, they say, in reply to the remarks made to him, observed, "My men have acted like women, my women like men!"

[Herodotus goes on to report that Mardonius, Xerxes' top general, advised the king to return home to Persia and to leave him in Greece with an infantry force to defeat the Greeks.]

8.101. Xerxes, when he heard Mardonius's words, felt a sense of joy and delight, like a man who is released from his worries. Telling Mardonius that he would consider his advice and then let him know which plan he preferred, Xerxes proceeded to consult with the chief men among the Persians. Since Artemisia previously had shown herself to be the only person who knew what was best to do, he decided to send for her to advise him now. As soon as she arrived, he sent away all the rest, both advisers and bodyguards, and said to her, "Mardonius wishes me to stay and attack the Peloponnese. My Persians, he says, and my other land forces are not to blame for the disasters that our army has suffered. He says that my forces would very gladly give me proof of this. He therefore urges me either to stay and act as I have said or to let him select 300,000 of my troops—with whom he promises to bring Greece under my rule—while I myself leave with the rest of my forces and withdraw into my own country. You, therefore, since you gave me such wise advice in telling me to avoid a naval battle, now also advise me on this matter, and tell me which of the two plans I ought to follow for my own good."

8.102. The king asked for Artemisia's advice in this way, and these are the words with which she answered him: "It is hard, my king, to give the best possible advice to one who asks for it. Nevertheless, as your affairs now stand, it seems to me that you would be right to return home. As for Mardonius, if he prefers to remain and promises to do as he has said, then by all means leave him behind, with the troops that he desires. If his plan succeeds and he defeats the Greeks, as he promises, it will be your victory, master, because your slaves will have accomplished it. If, on the other hand, things turn out opposite to his wishes, we will endure no great loss, so long as you are safe and your household is in no danger. The Greeks, too, while you are alive and your household flourishes, must be prepared to fight a great many battles for their freedom. If, on the other hand, Mardonius fails, it makes no difference—they will have won a very small triumph—a victory over one of your slaves! Remember also, you go home having accomplished the purpose of your expedition—you burned Athens!"

Xerxes asked Artemisia for advice.

8.103. Artemisia's advice pleased Xerxes greatly, for she had exactly expressed what he was thinking. I, for my part, do not believe that he would have remained in Greece even if all his advisers, both men and women, had united to urge him to stay, so great was the fear that he felt. As it was, he praised Artemisia and entrusted certain of his children to her care, ordering her to take them to Ephesus;[5] he had been accompanied on the expedition by some of his sons from secondary wives.

8.104. At this time, he also sent away one of his main eunuchs, a man named Hermotimus, from Pedasus,[6] who was ordered to look after these sons. The Pedasians inhabit the region above Halicarnassus. It is said that in their country, the following circumstance happens: When some misfortune is about to strike any of their neighbors within a certain time, the priestess of Athena in their city grows a long beard. This has already taken place on two occasions.

8.105. The Hermotimus of whom I spoke above was, as I said, a Pedasian. Of all men whom we know, he took the cruelest revenge on the person who had done him an injury. He had been made a prisoner of war, and when his captors sold him, a certain Panionius, a native of Chios who made his living in a very dirty business, bought him. Whenever Panionius could buy any boys of unusual beauty, he made them eunuchs. Taking them to Sardis or Ephesus, he sold them for large sums of money, because the barbarians value eunuchs more than other people, regarding them as more trustworthy. Panionius, who made his living by the practice, had treated many slaves in this way. Among them was this Hermotimus whom I have mentioned. However, Hermotimus also had some good luck: After a while, he was sent away from Sardis, together with other gifts, as a present to the king. Soon Xerxes valued him more highly than all his eunuchs.

8.106. When the king was on his way to Athens with the Persian army and stayed for a time at Sardis, Hermotimus happened to make a business trip into Mysia. There, in a district that is called Atarneus but belongs to Chios, he happened to meet up with Panionius. Recognizing him at once, Hermotimus began a long and friendly talk with him, during which Hermotimus counted up the numerous blessings he was enjoying thanks to Panionius's actions. He promised Panionius all kinds of favors in return if he would bring his household to Sardis and live there. Panionius was overjoyed and, accepting the offer, soon

---

[5] A city on the coast of Turkey.
[6] A town in northwestern Turkey, near the Hellespont.

showed up there with his wife and children. Then Hermotimus, when he had got Panionius and all his family into his power, addressed him in these words: "You, who make a living by fouler deeds than anyone else in the whole world, what wrong did I or any of my family do to you or your family, that you made me the nothing that I now am? Ah! Surely you thought that the gods paid no attention to your crimes. But they in their justice have delivered you, the doer of unrighteousness, into my hands. So you cannot complain about the vengeance that I am determined to take on you."

After these reproaches, Hermotimus commanded the four sons of Panionius to be brought to him and forced their father to make them eunuchs with his own hand. Unable to resist, he did as Hermotimus required. Then his sons were made to treat him in the very same way. So in this way, divine vengeance and Hermotimus came to Panionius.

6

Ending Stories: Cruelty and Revenge on Both Sides

These passages end Herodotus's book. They are two stories of cruelty and revenge, followed by a final anecdote about Cyrus, the founder of the Persian Empire in the sixth century BCE. The first story reports brutal intrigues in the household of King Xerxes of Persia, while the second describes Greek action against a Persian outpost remaining in Greek territory after the Persian Wars. Could the concluding position of these passages be meant to suggest that history shows this sort of evil to be universal? What does Herodotus's inclusion of women as main agents in the first story imply about their capacity for brutal behavior? Since the second story involves Xanthippus, the father of Pericles, Athens's political leader during the time Herodotus was writing, what message might Herodotus have been trying to send to the Greeks of his own time about their capacity for both glorious achievements and wrongdoing? Finally, note his treatment of the subject of luxury and excess in the anecdote about Cyrus's advice to the Persians.

From Herodotus, *The Histories*, bk. 9, secs. 107–22.

107. ... During the Persians' march home, Masistes, son of King Darius, who happened to have seen the Persian defeat by the Greeks [at Mycale,[1] in western Turkey, in 479 BCE], got into an argument with Xerxes' general Artayntes and verbally abused him. Worst of all, he said that a woman would have been a better leader than Artayntes and that he deserved the harshest possible punishment for the damage he had done to the king's household. [To call a man "worse than a woman" is the biggest insult of all for Persian men.] Having listened to this abuse, Artayntes in a rage drew his sword, ready to kill Masistes. But Xenagoras, a man from Halicarnassus, happened to be standing behind Masistes and, seeing him lunging forward, grabbed him around the waist, lifted him into the air, and threw him to the ground. This swift reaction gave Masistes' bodyguards enough time to surround him for protection. Xenagoras's actions pleased not only Masistes but also King Xerxes, for saving his brother. Xerxes rewarded Xenagoras by making him the ruler of the entire region of Cilicia. Nothing else remarkable took place on the march, and everyone reached Sardis in safety. There they met up with Xerxes, who had been staying in Sardis ever since he lost the sea battle [at Salamis in 480 BCE] and fled from Athens.

108. Since Xerxes had been in Sardis, he had fallen in love with Masistes' wife, who also happened to be there. He sent her messages, but she did not give in. He did not dare force her because she was his brother's wife. She knew this was so, and therefore she could hold out against his advances. Xerxes, with no other approach available, arranged for his son Darius to marry the daughter of Masistes, calculating that this would give him a better chance to get to the wife. Xerxes announced their engagement in the customary way and left for his capital in Susa in Persia. When he arrived, he received the young woman into his household as his son's bride—and then he changed his mind. Forgetting his passion for the bride's mother, he transferred it to Masistes' daughter—she who was now the wife of his son Darius. This time he got his way. The daughter's name was Artaynte.

109. Eventually, this affair was discovered in the following way. Amestris, Xerxes' wife, wove a large and distinctive multicolored robe that she gave him as a present. Pleased with his gift, Xerxes put it on and went to visit Artaynte. Delighted by their lovemaking, he told her to ask him for anything she wanted as a reward and promised she could

---

[1]Historians customarily refer to the "Battle of Mycale," although, technically speaking, Mycale is the name of the mountain range on the peninsula in southwestern Turkey where the battle took place along the shore.

have it. Artaynte, for whom, along with her entire family, things were destined to end badly, said to Xerxes, "Will you give me whatever I ask for?" Thinking that she would ask for anything other than what she did, Xerxes swore an oath that he would keep his promise. Since he had sworn, she fearlessly asked for the robe. Xerxes tried everything not to give it to her, for the sole reason that he was afraid of Amestris, who was already suspicious. He dreaded her getting proof of what was going on. He tried to give Artaynte cities of her own, unlimited quantities of gold, even an army for her to command by herself (this was a characteristically Persian gift). His attempts at persuasion failed, and he had to give her the robe. Artaynte was overjoyed; she loved wearing it.

110. Amestris, of course, discovered that Artaynte had the robe, but knowing what had happened did not make her angry with Artaynte. Amestris suspected that her mother was responsible, so she planned to destroy Masistes' wife. She waited for her husband, King Xerxes, to host the Royal Banquet (a meal prepared once a year for the king's birthday; the Persian word for it is *tucta*, which means "perfect" in Greek; it is the only day in the year when the Persian king washes his head and gives presents to the Persians). Waiting for that day, Amestris asked Xerxes for her present—and she asked for Masistes' wife. Xerxes thought it was awful that she asked for this present and did not want to give it, not only because he would be handing over his brother's wife but also because she was not responsible for what had happened. And he knew why his wife was making this request.

111. In the end, however, when Amestris kept pressing him and since Persian custom concerning the Royal Banquet said that no request that was put to the king at the meal could be refused, Xerxes very unwillingly agreed. He gave Masistes' wife to Amestris, telling her to do as she wished. He then called in his brother and said, "Masistes, you are Darius's son and my brother, and in addition you are one good man. Don't stay married to your present wife; I am going to give you my daughter. Marry her; I don't approve of your staying married to your current wife. Don't keep her as your wife."

Masistes, amazed at what Xerxes had said, replied, "Oh master, this is not a good idea that you are telling me, giving orders concerning my wife, who bore me sons who are now young men and daughters, one of whom you had marry your son, and who really suits and pleases me. You are ordering me to divorce her and marry your daughter? I, my king, have high respect for your daughter, but I am not going to divorce my wife or marry her. Do not force me to do this,

I am begging you! Some other man no less worthy than I will appear for your daughter. Let me stay married to my wife."

This reply made Xerxes furious. "All right, Masistes," he said. "This is what you have made happen: I am not going to give you my daughter to marry, and you are not going to have a minute more married to your wife! That way you can learn to accept a present that is given to you." When Masistes heard this, he ran out of the room, shouting, "Master, you haven't destroyed me yet!"

112. In the meantime, while Xerxes had been talking to his brother, Amestris had sent for the king's guards and had Masistes' wife horribly mutilated. Her breasts were cut off and thrown to the dogs, and her nose and her ears and her lips, and her tongue was torn out. Then she was sent home in this horribly mutilated condition.

113. Masistes had not yet heard what had been done, but he suspected something bad was in the works, so he hurried home. When he saw that his wife had been ruined, he immediately made plans with his children and set off to Bactria with his sons and some others, with the idea of starting a rebellion in the empire's Bactrian province and doing as much harm as possible to the king's affairs. He would have done it, it seems to me, if he had gotten away to the Bactrians and the Sacians, because those peoples loved him and he was the provincial governor of Bactria. But Xerxes learned of his plan and sent armed men after him. They killed him on the road, along with his sons and all his soldiers. So this is what happened concerning Xerxes' love and Masistes' death.

114. As for the Greeks who had set out from Mycale [after their victory there in 479 BCE] for the Hellespont, at first bad winds delayed them at the harbor of Leutas, but then they reached Abydos and discovered that Xerxes' temporary bridge had already been broken apart. They thought the bridge was still intact and had come to Abydos especially to destroy it. Under the circumstances, Leotychidas and the Peloponnesians thought the best thing was to sail home to Greece, but the Athenians and their commander Xanthippus stayed behind to try to take the Chersonese peninsula. So after the Peloponnesians had left, they crossed the strait from Abydos and began a siege of Sestos.

115. This place had the strongest defensive wall in the region, and as soon as people heard that the Greeks were present in the Hellespont, they poured into Sestos from the surrounding areas. Among them was Oeobazus, a Persian who had been in Cardia, where he had transported the cables used to build the bridge across the strait. The local Aeolian Greeks held Sestos, but many Persians were there, too, along with a large crowd of their allies.

116. Xerxes' provincial governor ruling this region was Artayktes, a Persian who was cunning and cruel. When Xerxes was leading his invasion against Athens, Artayktes had used trickery to get hold of the riches of Protesilaus, son of Iphiclus, which were at Elaeus in the Chersonese, where the tomb of that hero is located, in the midst of a sanctuary. This treasure included great riches, gold and silver drinking cups, bronze, clothing, and many other things that people had presented as offerings at the hero's tomb. Artayktes stole all of it, with the king's permission. He tricked Xerxes by saying, "Master, there is a house here that belonged to a Greek, who led an army against your territory and was killed, as he well deserved. Give me his house, so that people will know not to attack your land." By saying these things, he was easily going to convince Xerxes to give him the man's house, because the king had no idea he was being deceived. Artayktes had a point in saying that Protesilaus had led an attack on the king's land: The Persians consider all of Asia to belong to them and to whoever is reigning as their king. After the king made the gift, Artayktes brought the treasure from Elaeus to Sestos and converted the sanctuary into a farm. Whenever he visited Elaeus, he had sex with women in the sanctuary's holy room. At this point, the Athenians had Artayktes blockaded in Sestos. He had not made preparations to resist a siege and had not expected the Greeks to arrive; they therefore caught him off guard.

117. When the siege stretched on into autumn, the Athenian troops became unhappy as a result of being away from home for so long and their inability to storm Sestos's fortification wall. They therefore asked their commanders to lead them back home. The generals replied that they would not do that before they either took the town or the Athenian democratic government recalled them. So the soldiers had to endure the current conditions.

118. The people under siege in the town were already in the worst possible condition. They had to boil the leather straps from their bed frames for something to eat. When they had no more even of these, the Persians with Artayktes and Oeobazus got away during the night, climbing down at the back of the city wall, where the fewest enemy troops were. When daylight came, the people from the Chersonese in Sestos signaled from their towers to the Athenians to let them know what had happened and then opened the city gates. The majority of the Athenian troops set off after the runaways, while the rest took over the town.

119. The Apsinthian Thracians captured Oeobazus when he fled into Thrace and killed him as a sacrifice to their local god, Pleistorus, according to their custom. The others with him they killed in a different way. Those who had run away with Artayktes had left a little later, and they were caught close to Aegospotami. They resisted fiercely for quite a while, but they all ended up dead or captured. The Greeks tied them up and brought them back to Sestos, including Artayktes and his son.

120. The people of the Chersonese say that one of the guards of these prisoners saw an omen while he was cooking salted fish: The preserved fish, while being cooked over the fire, began to jump around and quiver, as if they had just been pulled out of the water. Everyone crowded around amazed, but when Artayktes saw this omen, he called to the man cooking the fish, "Athenian stranger, don't be afraid of this omen. It has nothing to do with you. It's Protesilaus of Elaeus giving me a sign that he may be as dead as a salted fish, but he still has power from the gods to take revenge on the one who treated him unjustly. I am now ready to pay compensation for the treasures I took from his shrine and dedicate it to him as a god, in the amount of a hundred talents, and I will give the Athenians eleven thousand pounds of silver if only my life and the life of my son will be spared."

His promise did not persuade Xanthippus, the Athenian commander. The people of Elaeus wanted revenge for Protesilaus and asked Xanthippus to execute Artayktes. Xanthippus had the same idea. They transported Artayktes down to the shore of the Hellespont where Xerxes had built his bridge across the strait—or, as some people say, they took him to a hill above the town of Madytus—and they hung him up, nailed to a plank. Then they stoned his son to death before his eyes.

121. After they had done this, they sailed back to Greece, taking with them lots of booty, above all the woven cables used to make the bridge. They were going to hang up the cables on the walls in the gods' shrines as a thank offering and memorial for their victories. Nothing more besides these events happened during this year.

122. This Artayktes who was nailed up to a board had an ancestor named Artembares, who had made an argument to the Persians that they enthusiastically agreed with and took to King Cyrus in the following words: "Since Zeus has given domination to the Persians, and to you among men, Cyrus, by defeating Astyages, listen to this. Since we possess a small and rugged land, let's change our location from this one, so we can have a better place. There are many nearby, and many others farther away. If we seize one of them, we will be much more amazing. It is appropriate for men who rule to do this sort of thing. When will there be a better time than when we rule many people and all of Asia?"

When Cyrus heard this, he did not regard it as a wonderful argument. He told them to go ahead, but he warned them that they should be prepared not to be rulers any longer and instead to be ruled, because soft men grow from soft countries. It is not possible for the same land to produce awesome crops and men who are good at war. As a result, the Persians agreed and got up to go home, defeated by Cyrus's thinking. They chose to go on living in a painful land and rule rather than to farm lush plains and live as slaves to other people.

Sima Qian, talks about what he does, and how he does history.

Herodotus -

Sima Qian, *The Records of the Historian*

7

Castration as the Price of Writing History: Sima Qian's Autobiographical Letter to Ren An

The historian Ban Gu (32–92 CE) included in his History of the Han Dynasty *(Han shu) this letter that Sima Qian wrote ca. 91 BCE to his friend Ren An when the latter was accused of disrespecting Emperor Wu. The emperor later had Ren An executed. In this letter, Sima Qian describes how he endured his own punishment of castration by the emperor so that he could continue the historical work that he had promised his father he would complete. The document highlights loyalty to parents in ancient Chinese culture, the notion of courage and cowardice, and how Sima Qian regarded his role in writing history.*

Dear Shaoqing,[1] my close friend:

Some time ago, you kindly sent me a letter advising me to be careful in my dealings with people, urging that it was my duty to recommend good men of quality and worth [for imperial positions]. Your concern was sincere and kind, but you might be disappointed in thinking that I have not heeded your words but instead have followed the advice of ordinary people. I assure you that I would not have dared to do so. Worthless and old creature that I am, I have heard of the teachings handed down from great men of earlier times. Yet I always remember that I am a mere mutilated body dwelling in degradation, that anything I try to do will merely meet with disapproval, and that

[1] Another name for Ren An.

Ban Gu, *Han shu*, chap. 62.

my efforts to help others would only do them harm. Therefore, I exist in sadness and sorrow, with no one to talk to.

There is an old saying, "For whose sake do you do what you do? Who will listen to you?" After Zhongzi Qi died, Bo Ya never played his lute again.[2] Why? Because a man acts for a friend who understands him and a woman wears makeup for an admirer who appreciates her beauty. But one like myself, whose body is now missing an essential part, can never lay claim to glory, even if I had qualities like Lord Sui's pearl and Bian He's jade,[3] or even if my actions were like those of Xū You or Bo Yi [see Document 11]. In fact, all my activity can win me no glory, only humiliation and ridicule.

I should have replied to your letter, but I had to serve the emperor on a trip to the east, and I felt pressure from some petty business of my own. The time we had together was short, and I was too busy to find a moment to tell you all that I really felt. Now that you, Shaoqing, have been accused of such an unimaginable crime and the days and months have slipped by, we are already in the last month of winter, and I am forced to go to Yong[4] to serve the emperor. If you should suddenly meet with what cannot be disguised by euphemism, it would mean that I would have no chance to tell you of all my bitterness and sorrow. Then, in the long journey hereafter, your spirit would forever feel secret resentment against me. So I beg you: Let me explain my unworthy ideas, and please do not blame me for being so late in answering.

I have heard that dedication to one's own moral training is the way to win wisdom, that delight in giving to others is the beginning of kindness, and that giving as well as accepting demonstrates one's sense of responsibility properly. I have also heard that being able to feel shame or disgrace determines one's courage and that making a name for oneself is the ultimate purpose of one's behavior. Only when one possesses these five qualities can he be trusted in the world and rank among the company of morally superior men. Therefore, no disaster can overcome a man if he craves no secret desires or monetary gains. No grief can be more painful than a broken heart, nor is there any deed more hideous than bringing shame on one's own ancestors. As for disgrace, none can ever be greater than the "palace punishment."[5] It is not the viewpoint of one generation alone, but rather has long been the belief,

---

[2] Bo Ya was a famous musician, and Zhongzi Qi was the only person whom he believed truly understood the ambition and significance of his playing.

[3] Precious items of legendary perfection.

[4] A location where the emperor performed sacrifices.

[5] Castration.

that it is improper to associate with a man who has undergone such punishment. When Duke Ling of Wei rode in the same carriage with the eunuch Yong Qu, Confucius departed for Chen. When Shang Yang obtained an audience with the king through the eunuch Jing Jian, Zhao Liang's heart turned cold. When the eunuch Zhao Tan rode in the emperor's carriage, Yuan Si changed color from shame.[6] To be associated with eunuchs has always been shameful since ancient times. If ordinary people despise associating with them, how much more so would gentlemen of virtue and feeling? Today the imperial court may be in need of good people, but how can I, something left over from the knife and saw, be worthy to recommend to the emperor the finest and most worthy men for his service?

Only because of my father's work, which has been passed on to me, have I been allowed for some twenty years to wait for my punishment alongside the wheel of the royal carriage.[7] I am quite aware that, first of all, I could not display my loyalty or inspire real confidence in serving our enlightened sovereign, and I could not gain a name for cleverness in planning or for superior ability. Second, I could not perform service to take care of shortcomings or supply what is lacking in imperial rule by promoting and recommending men of virtue and talent or bringing to light any good men who are living in seclusion. In dealing with foreign policy matters, I have had no command of troops, captured no townships, and fought on no battlefields. No glories of generals slain or enemy flags seized have ever been mine. At the lowest level, I have not, by doing my daily labor, achieved a high position or obtained a high salary that would secure benefits and favors for my family and friends. I have not succeeded in any one of these four areas of service. From this, it is obvious that I am worthless and tolerated at court by mere chance. At an earlier time, I, too, took my place among the lower officials and participated in the minor deliberations of the outer court. If I could not then introduce any great concepts or present any big ideas, now, when I am no more than a flunky sweeping the paths, mutilated and ranked among the lowly and insignificant, if I try to lift my head and look lordly by expressing my judgment on right and wrong, would I not show contempt for the court and bring shame to the current men of distinction? A man like me, what can I say, what can I say? How miserable!

---

[6]These are examples of the insult felt by those who had to be in the presence of castrated men.

[7]This phrase means "to serve the emperor."

It is not easy to know the beginning and the end of things. As a young man, I thought that I had unlimited spirit and ability, but as I grew up, I achieved no recognition in my village and district. But because of my ancestors, His Majesty graciously allowed me to offer my limited ability and to move around in the inner parts of the palace. I then thought to myself that a man with a bowl over his head could never see the heavens. Therefore, I severed all connections with my acquaintances and completely neglected all my family affairs. Day in and day out, the only thing I could think of was how to utilize my poor talents and strength fully to carry out my official duties with a single-minded passion, trying to win the favor and patronage of His Majesty.

But, destroying all my hopes, something terrible occurred because of a terrible misunderstanding! Although Li Ling[8] and I served together at the same time, we were never close, our likes and dislikes were different, we never even drank a cup of wine together, and we never shared the joys of close friendship. But I saw that he was a man of superior ability, loyal to his parents, trustworthy with associates, honest in matters of money, and fair and just in giving and taking. If a problem arose about status, he was prepared to yield, respectfully and modestly, and he would choose to overlook his own safety to attend to state emergencies. His mind was always like that, and I believed him to be one of the finest men in the nation. A subordinate who faced squarely ten thousand deaths without regard to his own life in order to rescue his master from disaster—that type of subject is indeed rare. But then he made just one wrong move, when all the officials whose only consideration was to save themselves and to protect their own wives and children competed in exaggerating his shortcomings. This really broke my heart!

Li Ling had hardly five thousand men under his command, yet they marched deep into the land of the barbarians.[9] They advanced all the way to the enemy's court, and at this point it was just like dangling bait in front of a tiger's jaws. They challenged the barbarians' horde of millions in more than ten days of fighting, and the enemy fell in disproportionate numbers. Those who tried to rescue their dead and wounded could not even save themselves, while their chieftains in their fur and wool robes trembled with fear. Then the whole country, including the powerful Left and Right Wise Kings,[10] as well as every

---

[8]Emperor Wu's general defeated by the Xiongnu.
[9]The Xiongnu (see Document 14). The Chinese regarded all the nomadic peoples on the frontiers as culturally inferior.
[10]Ruling leaders of the Xiongnu.

bowman, was summoned to participate in the battle. Their entire nation arose together to surround Li Ling and his men, who had fought their way for hundreds of miles already. They had shot all their arrows, the roads were blocked, and they had no way out. Their relief forces failed to come, and their casualties piled up in heaps. But with one shout, Li Ling encouraged his men to stand, and they all rose to his cry, even though they were drenched in blood and choked on their tears. They kept on pulling their empty bows to fight the enemy's naked blades. Turning northward, they fought to the death!

Before Li Ling was defeated, a messenger had come to report his attack, and all the dignitaries in the Han court toasted the emperor's health. But a few days later, the news of the defeat arrived, which made the emperor lose his appetite and become agitated during deliberations of the court. The dignitaries were in disarray, anxiety, and fear. Observing the emperor's grief and distress, I dared to forget about my lowly position and sincerely did what I could in my earnest ignorance. I believed that Li Ling had always shared his men's hardships and scarcities and that he could command the loyalty of his troops even in the face of death, which was something unique to him—not even the famous generals of ancient times could surpass him. Though he had been taken captive, his intention [in not fighting to the death] must have been to [stay alive] so that he could await an opportunity to repay what he owed the Han. Nothing could now be undone concerning what had happened, but those whom he had previously defeated constituted a sufficient accomplishment to make him a famous hero in the empire.

It was my intention to make this argument, but I had no way to express it. Then it so happened that I was summoned and questioned, so I made use of the opportunity and spoke highly of Li Ling's accomplishments, hoping to set the emperor's mind at ease and stop the malicious comments made by others. However, I was not able to be convincing, and the enlightened emperor did not feel persuaded. Instead, he believed that I was slandering the second-in-command General and making excuses for Li Ling's behavior. So I was put into jail. I had no chance to demonstrate the depth of my loyalty. In the end, I was convicted of having deceived and misled the emperor. My family was poor, and I did not have the money to buy my freedom. None of my acquaintances could save me, and not any of those close to me could utter a word on my behalf. I am not made of wood or stone. Alone with jailers as my only company, hidden in the depth of a prison cell, to whom could I complain? You now have your own experience to witness this yourself, but was there anything at all, do you think, that I had done wrong, Shaoqing? Li Ling surrendered alive, ruining the reputation of his family. I, too, went into the silkworm chamber, where castration is performed, becoming a laughingstock for the whole world to see. What misery! What misery!

It is not easy to explain things in a few words to ordinary people. My ancestor[11] had no accomplishments that entitled him to receive an investiture of split tally and the red charter.[12] He dealt with astronomy and the calendar, which are similar [in status] to divination and worship of the spirits. He was kept for the sport and amusement of the emperor, treated the same way as actors and court jesters, and scorned by his vulgar contemporaries. If I had accepted the legal judgment and been executed, it would not have made any more difference than a single hair falling off nine oxen. I was nothing but an ant to them. The world would not rank me among those who had died for their ideals, but would believe that my wisdom had been exhausted and my crime too severe, so that I could not escape my penalty and eventually met my death. Why? Because in their opinion, it was all due to my own past bad deeds that this had come upon me.

A man must die once. That death may be as weighty as Mount Tai[13] or light as a feather. The difference lies in what is accomplished by dying. Above all, a man must not bring shame to his ancestors. Next, he must not bring shame to his own person, or to his reasoning and appearance, or to his spoken words. Next, he must not bring shame by bending in submission, or wearing prison clothing, or being flogged while locked in the stocks, or having a shaved head with his body in metal chains. Following that is the shame of mutilated flesh and amputated limbs.

But the lowest of all is the extreme penalty: the "punishment of rottenness," which is castration! The saying goes, "Punishments are not extended to the high officials."[14] This means that a gentleman must always be careful about his proper conduct. When a fierce tiger lives deep in the mountains, all beasts tremble with fear, but when it is trapped in the cage, it wags its tail to beg for food, for it has been little by little broken in spirit and subdued. Therefore, if you mark out a

---

[11]Here he is referring specifically to his father.
[12]Indications of a person's noble status bestowed for important service to the dynasty that could provide protection against punishment.
[13]A place where special religious rites were held.
[14]That is, they are expected to commit suicide rather than be executed.

prison cell on the ground, a gentleman will not enter it. If you fashion a piece of wood to represent the warden, he will not speak to it in his own defense. He can make up his mind to show who he is [by committing suicide]. But let him cross his hands and feet to receive the shackles and rope, let him expose his flesh to receive the blows of the rod, hide him away in an enclosed cell, and he will knock his head on the ground when he sees the warden, and he will start panting in terror when he catches sight of the guards. Why? It is the natural outcome of being overcome by terrible power. Anyone reduced to such a condition who says there is no dishonor in it is faking and deserves no respect.

And yet the earl of the west was held prisoner in Youli. Li Si, the minister, suffered all five punishments. Even the prince of Huaiyin had to endure the stocks in Chen. As for Peng Yue and Zhang Ao, who had been enthroned as rulers, one went in chains to prison, the other to death. The marquis Zhou Bo executed the entire Lü clan, and his power surpassed that of the five earls, but he was imprisoned in a dungeon awaiting death. Wei Qi, a great general, wore prisoner's clothing and was tied up head, hands, and feet. Ji Bu became a slave of the Zhu clan. Guan Fu endured dishonor under house arrest.[15] All these men reached the position of lords of smaller principalities,[16] generals, or ministers, and their fame spread to neighboring lands. But when they were accused and sentence was passed on them, they did not even attempt to settle the matter with their own hands by committing suicide. In the dust and filth of bondage, it has always been the same, no matter if it is the past or the present. How can a man avoid shame under such circumstances? Thus one can see that bravery and cowardice are only matters of circumstance; strength and weakness depend on the situation. This is for sure, and there is no reason to doubt it at all!

Furthermore, if a man does not decide to settle things quickly outside the law but waits, he will soon sink lower and lower, until he lies beneath the whip and lash. If then he decides to save his honor by means of suicide, would it not be too late? This is why the ancients hesitated to administer punishments to officials. It is the nature of every man to love life and hate death, to think of his relatives, and to look after his wife and children. Only when he is motivated by higher ideals will this not be so, and there will be things he must do then.

---

[15]All these were once powerful people who suffered severe punishment.

[16]The name of this position is sometimes translated as "feudal lords," but that terminology seems to introduce inappropriate implications from European history.

Now I am very unfortunate to have lost my parents early and to be alone without any siblings. You, my dear Shaoqing, know that I would not let thoughts about a wife and children deter me from my decision. Yet a man of courage does not necessarily die for honor, and a coward can also aspire to do the right thing—he will then strive in any way he can!

I may have been fearful and weak in choosing life at any cost, but I also recognize the proper measure in how to act. How then could I endure the dishonor of sinking into prison bonds? If a captive slave girl can even take her own life, certainly someone like me could do the same when nothing else could be done. The reason I endured it in silence and did not refuse to be covered in filthy muck was because I could not bear the thought of leaving behind unfinished something of personal importance to me. I could not accept dying, if that meant that the high points of my writing were going to be lost to posterity.

In the past, there were many noble and wealthy people whose names disappeared with their deaths, and only the exceptional and the outstanding are known today. When Xi Bo was in prison, he expanded the *Classic of Changes* of Zhou.[17] When Confucius was destitute, he wrote the *Spring and Autumn Annals*. . . . Most of the three hundred poems in the book *The Telling of Disasters* were written when the sages of old poured out their anger and dissatisfaction. All these men felt anger in their hearts, for they were not able to accomplish what they wanted. Therefore, they wrote about past affairs to pass on their thoughts to future generations. Those who [because of their afflictions] could never hold office retired to write books to express their thoughts and soothe their rage, handing down their writings so they could show posterity who they were.

My humble self behaves no differently. Recently putting faith in my writings of no special talent, I have cast a universal net to gather together all the old traditions of the world that were scattered and lost. I have made an inquiry into the events of the past, testing what is true and what is false, connecting the end to the beginning and explaining the causes of success and failure and of rise and decay, in a total of 130 chapters.[18] I did all this desiring to research what is between heaven and earth and to clarify the changes of the past and the present, thereby completing a coherent explanation of the whole. Before my draft was complete, this calamity overtook me. It was my concern

---

[17] A collection of diagrams and sayings for predicting the future.
[18] The number of chapters in *The Records of the Historian*.

over this unfinished work that made me submit to the worst of all punishments without showing my rage. When I have truly completed this work, I shall store it on a famous mountain [not named here], to await those who will understand it and spread it throughout the countryside and all the capitals. When my work is known to the whole world, I will have paid the debt of my shame, and I will have no regret if I am killed ten thousand more times! However, this is something I can only confide to those who are intelligent, since it will be far too difficult for the ordinary crowd to comprehend.

It is not easy to live in poverty and disrespect, while the vulgar crowds multiply their slanderous gossips. I endured this misfortune only because of the words I spoke. I have brought upon myself the scorn and mockery of my own villagers, and I have soiled my ancestor's name. With what face can I stand again before my parents' grave? Even though a hundred generations might have passed away, my defilement will still be just as notorious. This is the thought that wrenches my bowels nine times a day. At home I am befuddled, as if I am completely lost. Outside the house, I do not know which way to go. Each time I think of this shame, sweat drips down my back, soaking my robe. I am now no more than a servant in the women's quarters. How I wish I could leave by myself, to hide away in some mountain cave. Therefore, I follow the ordinary crowd, floating and sinking together with them, bobbing up and down with the current vogue, sharing their delusion and craziness.

Now, my dear Shaoqing, you advise me to recommend worthy men and promote scholars. But would it not be at odds with my own view of things? Even if now I tried to recover glory and fame for myself by shaping refined words to explain my errors, it would have no effect whatsoever on ordinary folks, as they would not understand enough to believe me. Doing that would only create more shame for me. Therefore, I believe that only on the day of my death will the right and wrong be at last clarified.

I cannot possibly convey all that I would like to in this one letter. But I have attempted to set forth in brief my unworthy views.

8

The First Emperor of China: The Basic Annals of the Qin Dynasty

In the "Basic Annals" section of The Records of the Historian, *Sima Qian surveys the history of the different dynasties that ruled China from the earliest times to the Han dynasty in his own time. This excerpt is taken from one of the longest and most complicated chapters. Though focused on the famous First Emperor of Qin (Qin Shihuangdi; ruled as emperor 221–210 BCE), who fought long wars before finally making China into a unified state for the first time in 221 BCE, the chapter narrates the entire history of the short-lived Qin dynasty. This document foregrounds the issue of the power of history as a source of political criticism in imperial China. It also raises the question of whether the country was better off with its centralized imperial state and the emperor's ideals for ruling than when it consisted of divided kingdoms controlling separate, smaller regions.*

The man who became the First Emperor of the Qin dynasty was a son of Zhuang Xiang [king of Qin, r. 249–247 BCE] of the kingdom of Qin. When Zhuang Xiang was a diplomatic hostage from the kingdom of Qin being held captive in the kingdom of Zhao, he met Lü Buwei's concubine and liked her.[1] He took her for himself, and she gave birth in Handan,[2] to the son who would become the First Emperor of Qin in the first month of the forty-eighth year of King Zhao of Qin [259 BCE]. . . .

In the twentieth year [227 BCE] of the reign of the son of Zhuang Xiang, who had become king of Qin upon his father's death, Crown Prince Dan of the kingdom of Yan, fearing that the Qin army would march against his state, in desperation sent Jing Ke to assassinate the

---

[1]The rulers of the various states that made up China before it was unified as an empire often exchanged sons as hostages to make sure that both sides kept their diplomatic and military agreements. These so-called diplomatic hostages were treated well and not kept under close guard or imprisoned, so long as the agreements were honored.

[2]The capital of the kingdom of Zhao.

From Sima Qian, *The Records of the Historian*, chap. 6.

king of Qin [see Document 13]. When the king learned of the plot, he had Jing Ke torn limb from limb to serve as a warning. Then he sent Wang Jian and Xin Sheng to attack Yan. Yan and Dai called out their forces to fight the Qin army, but the Qin army defeated Yan west of the Yi River.

In the twenty-first year [226 BCE], Wang Ben attacked the Yan capital of Ji. Meanwhile, more and more troops were sent to reinforce Wang Jian's army, so that eventually he defeated the army of Crown Prince Dan, captured the city of Ji, and beheaded the crown prince. The king of Yan took control of the region of Liaodong and made himself the king there. Wang Jian asked permission to return to his home because he was old and sick. A revolt broke out in Xinzheng. There was a severe blizzard, with snow piling up to a depth of more than two feet....

In the twenty-sixth year [221 BCE], ...when Qin had for the first time united everything under heaven, the king of Qin instructed his chief minister and imperial secretary as follows: ..."As insignificant a person as I am, I assembled an army to punish the violent and the riotous. With the support of the sacred spirit of the ancestral temples, the six kings[3] have all submitted. Order is magnificently restored in everything under heaven. Now, if the ruler's title is not changed, there will be no means of praising these feats and achievements or of transmitting them to later generations. You are to discuss the imperial title."

Chief Minister Wang Wan, Imperial Secretary Feng Jie, Superintendent of Trials Li Si, and other officials all said, "In the past, the territory of the Five Emperors[4] was 250 miles square, and beyond this were the warring regions and the territory of the barbarians. Some of the subordinate lords came to court and some did not, for the Son of Heaven [the First Emperor of Qin] was unable to exercise control. Now Your Majesty raised a righteous army to punish the remaining lawbreakers and bring peace and order to everything under heaven, so that everywhere bordered by the seas has become our provinces and districts. The laws and ordinances have as a result become unified. This is something that has never once existed from remote antiquity onward and which the Five Emperors did not attain. Your servants have carefully discussed this with the scholars of broad learning. In antiquity, there existed the Heavenly Majesty, the Earthly Majesty, and the Supreme Majesty, with the Supreme Majesty the most highly

---

[3]This refers to the kings of China's regional kingdoms, whom he defeated.
[4]Mythological rulers of China in the third millennium BCE, before the first dynasty, the Xia, whose rule began at ca. 2205 BCE.

honored. Therefore, your servants, risking death, submit a venerable title and propose that the king should become 'the Supreme Majesty.' His commands should be 'decrees,' his ordinances should be 'edicts,' and the Son of Heaven should refer to himself as 'Zhen' (The One Apart from Others)." The king said, "Omit the word 'Supreme,' use 'Majesty,' and pick out the title 'Emperor' used from remote antiquity, so that the title will be 'Majestic Emperor.' The rest shall be as you suggest." And he decreed that this was permitted.

King Zhuang Xiang was to be posthumously honored as "the Supreme Majesty on High." The following decree was issued: "We have heard that in very ancient times, there were titles but no posthumous names. Somewhat later, there were titles, but when people died, they were provided with posthumous names that matched their conduct. If this is so, then the son passes judgment on the father, and the subject passes judgment on the ruler. This is quite pointless, and we will not adopt this practice in such matters. From now on, the law on posthumous names is abolished. I am the First Majestic Emperor, and later generations will be numbered, as the Second Generation, the Third Generation, right down to the Ten Thousandth Generation, and this tradition will continue without end."

Believing in the continuing cycle of succession of the Five Characterizations,[5] the First Emperor considered that as the Zhou dynasty had been endowed with the characterization of fire and now the Qin dynasty was replacing the Zhou power, Qin should adopt what fire does not overcome. Therefore, it was precisely at this moment that he prescribed the inauguration of the characterization of water [in his dynasty]. The beginning of the year was changed, and the court celebrations all started at the beginning of the tenth month. Black was made the dominant color in all garments, flags, and pennants. As far as number was concerned, they took six as the base for calculation, so that accounting units and judiciary caps were six inches long, carriages were six feet wide, six feet equaled a "step," and imperial carriages had six horses. The Yellow River[6] was renamed Excellent Water to initiate the characterization of water. Repression was intense, and everything was decided according to harsh law, which did away with humaneness, kindness, harmony, and righteousness. Only in this way

[5] Or "Phases" or "Essences." The respective characterizations of wood, fire, earth, metal, and water, when compared or put into competition with each other, were seen as representative of the process of change in human events.
[6] The northernmost of China's two main east-west waterways.

could it fit with the prescriptions of the Five Characterizations. And so the law was made rigorous, and criminals being imprisoned for long sentences were not pardoned. . . .

So the empire was divided into thirty-six districts, and a governor, an army commander, and an inspector were established for each district. They renamed the people "the black-headed ones," and there was a great feast for celebration. The weapons from everywhere under heaven were gathered together and brought to Xianyang.[7] They were melted down to make bells and other musical instruments made of bronze, as well as twelve statues of men all made of solid metal, each weighing ninety tons, to be set up in the courts and palaces. All weights and measures were regularized in a unified system, and the axle length of carriages was standardized. They standardized the characters used in writing. The land of the empire stretched eastward as far as the sea and Chaoxian, to the west as far as Lintao and Jiangzhong, to the south as far as the land where the doors of houses face north [to keep the hot sun from shining directly into the building].[8] In the north, they constructed defenses[9] along the Yellow River to form the frontier and along the Yin Mountains as far as Liaodong. One hundred and twenty thousand powerful and wealthy households from everywhere under heaven were transferred to Xianyang. All the temples, together with the Zhangtai and Shanglin gardens, were to the south of the Wei River. Every time Qin destroyed a subordinate state, a replica of its palaces and mansions was produced and built on the slope north of Xianyang, overlooking the Wei River to the south, while eastward from Yongmen as far as the Jing and Wei rivers there was a series of palaces, connecting walkways, and pavilions. To fill them, they installed the beautiful women, bells, and drums that they had obtained from the various states. . . .

In the twenty-eighth year [219 BCE], the First Emperor traveled eastward through his provinces and districts and ascended Mount Zhouyi. He set up a stone tablet, and after discussion with the various Confucian scholars of Lu, an inscription was carved on the stone praising the characterization of Qin. They also discussed the sacrifice to Heaven, the sacrifice to Earth, and the sacrifices to mountains and rivers. Next he climbed Mount Tai, set up a stone tablet, and performed the sacrifice to Heaven. As he descended the mountain, there

[7]The capital of the state of Qin.
[8]An indication of a very southern location, whose exact identity remains unknown.
[9]The Great Wall.

was a violent storm. He rested under a tree, which was consequently given the status of a fifth-rank noble. He performed the sacrifice to Earth at Liangfu. The stone tablet that he had set up was inscribed with the following words:

> When the Majestic Emperor came to the throne, he created regulations and made the laws intelligent, and his subjects cherished his instructions. In the twenty-sixth year of his rule, he for the first time unified everything under heaven, and there was none who did not submit. He personally made tours of the black-headed people in distant places, climbed this Mount Tai, and gazed all around at the eastern limits. His servants who were in attendance concentrated on following his footsteps, looked upon his deeds as the foundation and source of their own conduct, and reverently celebrated his achievements and excellence. As he exercises good government, his subjects produce suitable harvests, and everything has its laws and patterns. His great righteousness shines forth with its blessings, to be handed down to later generations, and they are to receive it with strict compliance without alteration. The Majestic Emperor respects wisdom, and once he pacified everything under heaven, he has never been lazy in governing it. Getting up early and going to bed late, he has instituted long-lasting benefits and has brought special glory to instructions and precepts. His maxims and rules spread all around, and everything far and near has been properly organized. Everyone receives the benefit of his wise ambitions. The noble and the common have been divided off and made clear, and men and women conform to standards of proper conduct and carefully fulfill their duties. Private and public are made clear and distinguished from one another, and nothing is not pure and clean, for the benefit of our heirs and successors. His influence will last to all eternity, and the decrees he passes down will be revered, and his solemn admonitions will be inherited forever. . . .

In the thirty-fourth year [213 BCE], judicial officials who had behaved improperly were banished either to build the Great Wall or to move to the territory of southern Yue. The First Emperor arranged a banquet in the palace at Xianyang, and the seventy scholars of broad learning came into his presence to wish him long life. The chief administrator of these scholars, Zhou Qing Chen, came forward to offer praises, saying, "At first, Qin territory hardly exceeded 250 miles on a side, but now thanks to Your Majesty's divine power and brilliant wisdom, the area within the seas has been restored to order and the barbarian tribes have been completely driven off. Whatever lands the sun and the moon shine over, there is no one who did not submit.

The subordinate states have been made into provinces and districts, everyone is content and happy, there is no worry about war or conflict, and this will be handed down for ten thousand generations. Ever since very ancient times, Your Majesty's authority and excellence have never been matched." The First Emperor was pleased.

Then the scholar of broad learning, Chun Yu Yue, a man from Qi, stepped forward and said, "Your servant has heard that the reason that the Yin and Zhou dynasties reigned for more than one thousand years was because they appointed their sons and younger brothers and successful officials as lords obliged to them, to provide branches and supports for themselves. Now that Your Majesty possesses everything within the seas, your sons and younger brothers are only private individuals. If you happen to have subordinates like Tian Chang or the six ministers,[10] there is no one who can offer support and assistance. How can you rescue each other? It is unheard of for anything to long survive that is not modeled on the past. Now Qing Chen is also flattering you to your face, to lead Your Majesty into making mistakes; thus he is not behaving like a loyal subject."

After the First Emperor issued his comments, Chief Minister Li Si said, "The Five Emperors did not repeat each other's behaviors, and the Three Dynasties[11] did not copy each other's ways, yet each achieved good government. It was not that they rejected each other's ways, but that times had changed. Now Your Majesty has created a great enterprise and constructed an achievement that will last for ten thousand generations, which is certainly not something that a foolish follower of Confucius could understand! Moreover, what Yue is referring to is just the activities of the Three Dynasties, and they surely are not worthy of being taken as precedents. In those times, the subordinate lords were in competition with each other to give a generous welcome to wandering men of learning.

"Now everything under heaven has been restored to order, while laws and ordinances are all derived from one single source. The common people at home put their effort into farming and handicrafts, while the public servants study the laws and prohibitions. At this time, all the scholars do not take the present as a model but instead study the past. Therefore, they reject the present generation and throw the black-headed people into confusion. As chief minister, your servant Li

---

[10]That is, murderous rebels who tried to overthrow their sovereign.
[11]The Xia, Shang, and Zhou, the legendary first dynasties, which ruled from the second millennium BCE to the time of the Qin dynasty in the third century BCE.

Criticism

Si speaks out at risk of death. In the past, everything under heaven was divided and in chaos, and nobody could unify it. It was for this reason that the subordinate lords became active together, and in their speeches they all spoke of the past to injure the present. They made a display of empty words to throw the truth into confusion. People preferred what they had learned in private in order to reject what their superiors had laid down. Now the Majestic Emperor has unified and taken possession of everything under heaven. You have distinguished white from black and established a single focus of adulation. But those who have studied privately collaborate with each other to reject the laws and teachings. When people hear ordinances proclaimed, everyone criticizes them in accordance with his own studies. Indoors they mentally reject them, and outside they make criticisms in the streets. They criticize their sovereign to make a reputation for themselves. They regard disagreements as highly valuable, and they lead the common people to fabricate slander. If such things are not prohibited, then the sovereign's power will decline above and factions will form below.

"To prohibit this would be expedient. Your servant requests that the records of the historians, except for those of Qin, be burned. Apart from those copies that the scholars of broad learning are responsible for in their official capacity, anyone anywhere under heaven who dares to possess and hide away the *Classic of Poetry*, the *Classic of Documents*, and the sayings of the Hundred Schools of Thought,[12] should hand them all over to a governor or commandant, and all this should be collected and burned. If there is anyone who dares to mention the *Classic of Poetry* or *Classic of Documents* in private conversation, he should be executed. Those who use the old and reject the new will be wiped out, together with their clans. Officials who see and become aware of such cases but do not report them should suffer the same penalty. If thirty days after the ordinance has been proclaimed, the books are not burned, then the culprit should be branded and sent to do forced labor on the walls. There should be exemption for books concerned with medicine, pharmacy, divination [procedures for telling the future], and horticulture. If anyone intends to make a study of the laws and ordinances, he should take the law officers as teachers."

The emperor issued a decree saying this was permitted.

[12]This expression refers to the many philosophical traditions of China before the Qin dynasty.

9

Born from a Dragon: The Origins of Gaozu, Founder of the Han Dynasty

In this excerpt from a long chapter in the "Basic Annals" section, Sima Qian narrates the rise and fall of Gaozu ("Exalted Ancestor"; r. 206–195 BCE), founder of the Han dynasty, which ruled during Sima Qian's lifetime. (Chinese emperors acquired different names to be used in different contexts. In modern works, Gaozu is often referred to as Liu Bang.) Notice how Sima Qian combines legend and morality tale to establish the ideals of proper dynastic rule, focusing on Gaozu's character and special destiny even before he fought his way to the throne. Notice also the section at the end that begins "The Grand Astrologer comments." In such concluding sections, which are common in The Records of the Historian, *Sima Qian comments on the significance of the people and events he has just written about.*

Gaozu came from the village of Zhongyang in the township of Feng in the district of Pei. His family name was Liu, while his courtesy name[1] was Ji. His father was called Taigong (Venerable Grandfather), his mother Liuao (Venerable Lady Liu). When Liuao was young, she once rested on the bank of a great marsh and dreamed that she had an encounter with a god. There was thunder and lightning, and it grew dark. Taigong went to look for her and saw a scaly dragon on top of her. Afterward she became pregnant and gave birth to Gaozu.

Gaozu was described as having a prominent nose and a broad forehead like a dragon, with beautiful whiskers and a beard. On his left thigh he had seventy-two black moles. He was kind and gracious to others, and he loved being generous and open-minded. He always had great plans, but he ignored the business and livelihood that the rest of his family members worked at. When he grew up, he took the examination to become an official and was made village head of the Si River precinct. He treated all other officials casually and even with disdain. He was fond of wine and women. He spent many hours at Venerable

---

[1]The designation indicating he came from a well-known family.

From Sima Qian, *The Records of the Historian*, chap. 8.

Lady Wang's or Old Aunt Wu's bar drinking on credit. When he got drunk and lay down to sleep, the women, to their great surprise, would often see a dragon there. Also, whenever Gaozu came to drink and spend time at their shops, they would be able to sell several times as much wine as usual. Because of such strange happenings, at the end of the year the old women would forgive Gaozu's debts and clear his account.

Gaozu happened to be in Xianyang doing unpaid compulsory labor for the government when the ordinary people were allowed to gaze upon the First Emperor of Qin. When Gaozu saw the emperor, he sucked in his breath and exclaimed, "That's it! A great man of ambition should be like this!"

Master Lü of Shanfu was a good friend of the magistrate of Pei, and to avoid a feud, he moved to Pei to be the magistrate's retainer. When the officials and the wealthy and influential people of Pei heard that the magistrate had a distinguished guest, they all came to pay their respects. Xiao He was the chief clerk in charge of gifts, and he announced that anyone coming to call should never bring a gift of less than one thousand cash,[2] or he would be seated below the main hall. Gaozu, who as a village head treated other officials with contempt, falsely wrote on his calling card, "With respects—ten thousand cash," although in reality he did not have a single coin on him. When the card was presented to Master Lü, he was so shocked that he sprang to his feet and rushed over to greet Gaozu at the door. Master Lü was very good at reading faces,[3] and when he saw Gaozu's face, he treated him with great honor and respect and led him in to be seated. Xiao He commented, "Gaozu talks big but achieves little." Gaozu, treating the other guests with disdain, took a seat of honor without hesitation.

When the drinking was nearly over, Master Lü looked at Gaozu, indicating that he should stay. So Gaozu continued to drink and stayed behind. Master Lü said to him, "I have been very fond of reading faces and have read many, but none was as distinguished as yours. Take good care of yourself, I beg you. I have a daughter whom I hope you will do me the honor of accepting [as your wife] to take care of you." When the party was over, Master Lü's wife was angry with him and said, "You have always wanted to idolize this girl and marry her to a nobleman of distinction. The magistrate of Pei is good to you and has asked for her, but you won't give your consent. How can you be so insane as to offer her to Gaozu?" Master Lü replied, "This is not the

---

[2]A large amount of copper coins.
[3]That is, predicting people's fates and fortunes from the shapes of their faces.

sort of thing that you women and children would know about." Eventually, he married his daughter to Gaozu. This daughter of Master Lü then became Empress Lü [see Document 10] and gave birth to Emperor Hui the Loyal Son and Princess Yuan of Lu.

While Gaozu was serving as village head, he once asked for home leave to visit his fields. At the time, Empress Lü, together with her two children, was in the fields pulling weeds. An old man passed by and asked her for something to drink. Empress Lü gave him some food as well. The old man examined her face and said, "Your Ladyship will become the most honored person in the world." She asked him to examine her children. Looking at her son [the future Emperor Hui], he said, "It is because of this boy that Your Ladyship will be honored," and when he examined the girl [Princess Yuan], he said that she, too, would be honored. After the old man was gone, Gaozu happened to appear from a building nearby. Empress Lü told him how the traveler, while passing by, had examined her and her children, predicting great honor for them all. When Gaozu asked where the man was, she said, "He cannot have gone far." Gaozu ran after the old man, and when Gaozu caught up with him, he questioned the man. The old man replied, "The lady and the little children I examined a while ago all resemble you. But when I examine your face, I find such worth that I cannot express it in words!" Gaozu thanked him, saying, "If it is really as you say, I will surely not forget your kindness!" But when Gaozu finally became honored, he could never discover where the old man had gone.

When Gaozu was serving as village head, he designed a hat fashioned from the outer bark of a bamboo tree and sent one of his officers, the bandit seeker, to Xie to have some hats made. He wore one from time to time. When he became honored, he wore it frequently. After that, it was always called "the Liu family hat."

While village head, Gaozu happened to escort a group of forced laborers to work at Mount Li, but many of the workers ran away while on the road. He figured that he was going to lose them all before the end of the trip, so when they reached the middle of a marsh west of Feng, he stopped to let them drink. Later, during the night, he loosened the laborers' shackles to free them, saying, "Go, all of you, and I, too, will go my own way from here." A dozen or so strong men among the forced laborers were willing to follow him. Tipsy from wine, Gaozu set out during the night and took a shortcut through the marsh. A man was told to walk ahead, but he returned to report, "There is a big snake blocking the path—we have to turn back." Now drunk, Gaozu said, "The strong man should march on—what would he fear?" So he stepped forward, drew his sword, and struck the snake, cutting it in two and clearing the way. He moved on for a mile or so, became very drunk, and lay down.

When those in the rear came to where the snake was, they found an old woman crying in the night. Someone asked her why, and the old woman said, "I was crying because someone killed my son." The man asked, "Why was your son killed?" The old woman said, "My son was the son of the White Emperor. He changed into a snake to block the way, but the son of the Red Emperor cut him in half.[4] That was why I cried." The man did not believe that the old woman was telling the truth, and he was about to punish her, when the old woman suddenly disappeared. The man caught up with Gaozu, who woke up and was informed about the old woman. The story secretly pleased Gaozu and made him think much of himself. His followers grew in greater awe of him day by day.

[The rest of the chapter describes the wars that Gaozu fought to become emperor and found the Han dynasty. It concludes with the following explicit comments by Sima Qian, who refers to himself as the Grand Astrologer.]

The Grand Astrologer comments: The governing of the Xia dynasty [ca. 2205–ca. 1766 BCE] was distinguished by good faith, but over time it deteriorated, to the point that small-minded people made it go out of control. Therefore, the men of the Shang dynasty [ca. 1766–ca. 1045 BCE], who took over rule from the Xia, emphasized respect. But respect deteriorated into ritual, so that the small-minded people turned it into superstition. For that reason, the people of the Zhou dynasty [ca. 1045–256 BCE], who succeeded the Shang, turned to knowledge of literature as a tool for governing. When this knowledge of literature deteriorated, the small-minded people made it meaningless. What was needed to combat this meaninglessness was a return to good faith, for the way of the Three Dynasties is cyclical: The end comes back to the beginning.

The knowledge of literature as a tool for governing definitely deteriorated further between the end of the Zhou dynasty and the Qin dynasty [221–207 BCE]. The government of Qin nevertheless did not change its policies. Instead, it added its own cruel punishments and rules. Was this not truly a serious mistake?

For this reason, when the Han dynasty reached its full power [206 BCE], it inherited the causes of decay of the previous dynasties.

---

[4]Colors were used to designate different ruling regimes and factions.

Despite this, it worked to improve things and make reforms, requiring people to exert themselves tirelessly. As a result, it finally achieved the order that Heaven dictates. Gaozu convened the court in the tenth month [to have his subordinates around the country pay their respects for the coming year]. The curtains and the top of his carriage were yellow, with plumes on the left side. He was buried in the place called Long Burial Mound.

10

A Woman in Power: Empress Lü

This chapter of the "Basic Annals" section focuses on Empress Lü (r. 188–180 BCE), raising the issue of gender relations in Han China and the appeal that power holds for women as well as men. It also brings to the fore the importance of family as a motive for action. Given the bloody violence that the empress employed to satisfy her ambition, why would Sima Qian offer a seemingly positive evaluation of her rule in "The Grand Astrologer comments" section? What conclusions might he have wanted his audience to reach?

Empress Lü was the consort of Gaozu from the time when he was still a commoner. She bore him Emperor Hui the Loyal Son and Princess Yuan of Lu. When Gaozu became king of Han, he took into his service Lady Qi of Dingtao, whom he loved dearly. She bore him a son, Liu Ruyi, king of Zhao, posthumously known by the name Yin. Emperor Hui was by nature weak and softhearted. Gaozu was convinced that the boy had an entirely different temperament from his own, and so he wanted to remove him from the position of heir apparent and instead make Ruyi, son of Lady Qi, his heir. "For Ruyi is just like me," he would say. Lady Qi, happy to be favored, frequently accompanied Gaozu on his trips going east of the pass. She kept weeping day and night, begging for her son to become heir apparent. Empress Lü, being well along in years, always stayed behind in the capital. She rarely saw the emperor, and they became more and more estranged. Ruyi was made king of Zhao and subsequently several times came

---

From Sima Qian, *The Records of the Historian*, chap. 9.

very near to replacing the future Emperor Hui as heir apparent. But because of the objections of the high officials and the strategy devised by Zhang, a noble of [the state of] Liu, the heir apparent was not removed from his position.

Empress Lü was a woman of very strong will. She aided Gaozu in the conquest of the empire, and many of the great ministers who were executed were the victims of her power. She had two older brothers, both of whom were generals. . . . In the twelfth year of his reign [195 BCE], Emperor Gaozu passed away in the Palace of Lasting Joy. The heir apparent, Hui, became emperor. . . .

Empress Lü intensely hated Lady Qi and her son, the king of Zhao. She gave orders for Lady Qi to be imprisoned in the Long Halls and summoned the king of Zhao to court. Three times messengers were sent back and forth, but the prime minister of Zhao, Zhou Chang, the noble of Jianping,[1] told them, "Gaozu entrusted the king of Zhao to my care, and he is still very young. Rumors have reached me that Empress Lü hates Lady Qi and wishes to summon her son, the king of Zhao, so that she can kill both of them. I do not dare to send the king! Moreover, he is ill and cannot obey the summons." Empress Lü was furious and proceeded to send a messenger to summon Zhou Chang himself. When Zhou Chang obeyed her order and arrived in Changan,[2] she dispatched someone to summon the king of Zhao once more. The king set out, but before he reached the capital, Emperor Hui, compassionate by nature and aware of his mother's hatred for the king of Zhao, went in person to meet him at the Ba River and accompanied him back to the palace. The emperor looked out for the boy and kept him by his side, eating and sleeping with him, so that although Empress Lü wished to kill him, she could find no opportunity.

In the first year of Emperor Hui's reign, . . . the emperor rose at dawn one morning to go out hunting, but the king of Zhao, being very young, could not get up so early. When Empress Lü heard that he was in the room alone, she sent someone to give him poison to drink. By the time Emperor Hui returned, the king of Zhao was dead. After this, Yu, the king of Huaiyang, was transferred to the position of king of Zhao. . . .

Empress Lü later cut off Lady Qi's hands and feet, plucked out her eyes, burned her ears, gave her a potion to drink that made her mute,

---

[1]The region that the emperor entrusted to Zhou Chang to control as his own property from which to draw income.

[2]The ancient capital city.

and had her thrown into the latrine, calling her the "human pig." After a few days, she sent for Emperor Hui and showed him the "human pig." Staring at her, he asked who the person was, and only then did he realize that it was Lady Qi. Thereupon he wept so bitterly that he grew ill, and for over a year he could not leave his bed. He sent a messenger to report to his mother, "No human being could have done such a cruel deed as this! Since I am your son, I will never be fit to rule the empire." From this time on, Emperor Hui gave himself up to wine each day and no longer took part in governing, and so his illness grew worse.

In the second year of Emperor Hui's reign [193 BCE], King Yuan of Chu and King Dao Hui of Qi came to court. In the tenth month, Emperor Hui held a banquet for the king of Qi that the empress attended. Because the king of Qi was his elder brother, Emperor Hui seated him in the place of honor and treated him with the courtesy customary among members of the same family. Empress Lü was furious at this and ordered two goblets to be prepared with poison and placed before the king of Qi. Then she instructed the king to rise and propose a toast. When he did so, Emperor Hui also rose and picked up the other goblet, intending to join in the toast. Empress Lü, terrified, rose from her own place and overturned Emperor Hui's goblet. The king of Qi grew suspicious and did not dare to drink any more. Pretending to be drunk, he left the banquet. Later, when he learned that the goblet had indeed contained poison, he began to fear that he would not be able to escape from the court at Changan. Shi, the internal secretary of Qi, spoke to the king, saying, "Empress Lü has only two children, the emperor and Princess Yuan of Lu. Now Your Majesty possesses over seventy cities, while the princess receives the revenue from only a very few. If you were willing to donate one province to the empress that could be assigned to the princess as her 'bath-town,'[3] then the empress would surely be pleased and you would have nothing more to fear." The king of Qi accordingly donated the province of Chengyang and honored the princess with the title "Empress Lü." Her mother, Empress Lü, accepted these honors with delight and held a banquet at the state residence of Qi.[4] When the drinking and rejoicing were over, she sent the king of Qi back to his kingdom. . . .

In the seventh year [188 BCE], Emperor Hui the Loyal Son died. Mourning was announced, and Empress Lü lamented, but no tears fell

---

[3]Property from which income would be derived for personal expenses.
[4]This was an official residence in the capital, which served as a kind of embassy for the subordinate states.

from her eyes. Zhang Piqiang, the son of the noble Zhang, was a page in the palace, and although he was only fifteen, he said to the prime minister, "Empress Lü had only this one son, Emperor Hui. Yet now that he has passed away, she laments but does not seem to express real grief. Can you solve this riddle, my lord?" The prime minister answered, "How would you explain it?" Zhang Piqiang said, "Emperor Hui left no grown sons, and so Empress Lü is afraid of you and the others. I would suggest now that you honor Lü Tai, Lü Chan, and Lü Lu[5] with the rank of general, put them in charge of the soldiers in the northern and southern garrisons, and allow the various members of the Lü family to enter the palace and take part in the government. If this is done, Empress Lü will feel more at ease, and you and the other ministers may be fortunate enough to escape disaster." The prime minister did as the boy suggested. Empress Lü was pleased, and her lamentations took on an air of genuine sorrow. This was the start of the Lü family's rise to power. A general amnesty was proclaimed in the empire, and in the ninth month . . . Emperor Hui was buried. The heir apparent succeeded to the throne and became emperor, paying his respects at the funerary temple of Emperor Gaozu.

In the first year, all orders issued from Empress Lü, and she called them "decrees," in the manner of an emperor. Then she began deliberations with the idea of making kings of the members of her own family, asking the Chancellor of the Right Wang Ling what he thought of such a step. "Emperor Gaozu killed a white horse and had us all swear, 'If anyone not of the Liu family becomes a king, the empire will unite in attacking him.' Now if members of the Lü family were to be made kings, it would be a violation of this agreement!" Empress Lü was displeased and consulted Chen Ping, the Chancellor of the Left, and Zhou Buo, the noble of Jiang. Zhou Buo and the others replied, "When Emperor Gaozu conquered the world, he made kings of his sons and younger brothers. Now that the empress is issuing decrees in the manner of an emperor, if she wishes to make kings of her brothers, we cannot see that there is any objection." Empress Lü was pleased and dismissed the court.

When the proceedings were over, Wang Ling began to berate Chen Ping and Zhou Buo. "Were you not present when Emperor Gaozu and the rest of us smeared our lips with the blood of the white horse and swore our agreement?" he said. "Now that Emperor Gaozu has passed away, Empress Lü has made herself ruler and wants to elevate the

---

[5]These were relatives of Empress Lü.

members of her family to be kings. All of you think perhaps you can ignore your oath and flatter the will of the empress. But how will you dare to face Emperor Gaozu in the world beneath?" "When it comes to opposing the ruler and speaking out in court," replied Chen Ping and Zhou Buo, "we are no match for you. But in preserving the altars of the dynasty and ensuring the continuation of the Liu family, it is possible that you are no match for us." Wang Ling had no answer to this. . . .

The daughter of the noble of Xuanping had been made queen, the wife of Emperor Hui. When the queen failed to bear a son, she pretended to be pregnant. Substituting an infant born to one of the emperor's ladies in waiting, she called it her own. Then she murdered the mother and installed the child as heir apparent. When Emperor Hui died, this child became emperor. As the emperor grew a little older, he began to hear rumors that his mother had been killed and that he was not the real son of Emperor Hui's wife. "What right had the queen to kill my mother and call me her son?" he declared. "I am not old enough now, but when I grow up, things will change!" Empress Lü heard of this, and she became worried for fear that he might start a revolt. She therefore locked him in the Long Halls and announced that the emperor was seriously ill. None of the officials were allowed to see him. Then Empress Lü proclaimed, "He who holds possession of the empire and rules the destinies of the multitude must shelter them like the heavens and support them like the earth. The ruler must bring peace to the people with a joyous heart, and the people in gladness must serve their ruler. When this joy and gladness mingle together, then the empire will be well governed. Now the emperor's illness has continued for a long time without stopping, so much so that he has lost his mind and become demented. He is not fit to carry on the imperial line and perform the sacrifices in the ancestral temples, and he cannot be trusted with the care of the empire. Let him be replaced!" . . .

The emperor was removed from his position, and Empress Lü had him secretly murdered. In the fifth month of the fourth year [184 BCE], . . . Yi, the king of Changshan, was made emperor, and his name was changed to Heng. The year was not designated as the first year of a new reign because Empress Lü was directing the government of the empire.

In the first month of the seventh year [181 BCE], Empress Lü summoned Yiu, the king of Zhao, to the capital. Yiu had taken a daughter of the Lü family as his queen, but he had no love for her and favored a concubine instead. The daughter of the Lü family, consumed with jealousy, left him and began to slander him to Empress Lü. She accused him of disloyalty and reported that he had said, "What right has the Lü family to become kings? When Empress Lü's days are over, I will certainly attack them!" The empress was furious, and for this reason she called the king of Zhao to the capital. When he arrived, she kept him at the state residence of Zhao and would not see him. She ordered the place surrounded by guards and refused to send him food. When some of the officials secretly sent him provisions, she had them immediately arrested and condemned to punishment.

When the king of Zhao was starving, he composed this song: "The Lü clan controls all affairs; the Liu clan is in peril. They have oppressed the nobles and forced this wife upon me, a wife who in her jealousy speaks pure evil of me. A slandering woman will undo the state, for those in power are blind. Though I lack loyal ministers, why should I cast away my kingdom? If I killed myself in the open fields, blue Heaven would speak the justice of my cause. Oh, it is too late for regret; it is better if I end it immediately. A king and yet to starve to death—who will pity one like me? The Lü clan has overturned justice; I call on Heaven for my revenge!"

The king of Zhao died while locked away. He was buried with the rituals for a commoner in the graveyard of the common people of Changan. On [March 4, 181 BCE], there was an eclipse of the sun, and the day grew dark. Empress Lü was upset by this event, and her heart grew uneasy. Turning to those about her, she said, "This has happened because of me!" . . .

Liu Hui, the king of Liang, was deeply disturbed by being transferred to the position of king of Zhao. Empress Lü had given him the daughter of Lü Chan to be his queen, and all of her attendants and ministers were members of the Lü family. They used their power in a completely arbitrary way and secretly spied on the king, so that he could do nothing as he wished. The king had a concubine whom he loved dearly, but the queen sent someone to poison her. The king, deeply aggrieved, composed in her memory a song in four stanzas and ordered his musicians to sing it. In the sixth month, he committed suicide. When Empress Lü received the news, she declared that he was guilty of abandoning his duties to his ancestral temples by committing suicide for the sake of a woman, and she deprived his heir of the royal title. . . .

During the third month [of 180 BCE], Empress Lü was returning from a sacrifice when, at the Zhi pass, she saw a creature in the form of a blue dog that seized her under her arm. It then suddenly disappeared. A diviner was called to interpret the incident, and it was determined that it was the manifestation of the angry spirit of Liu Ruyi, the king of Zhao. The empress soon grew ill from the wound under her arm. . . .

During the seventh month, Empress Lü's illness grew worse. She appointed Lü Lu, the new king of Zhao, as supreme commander of the army and ordered him to the northern garrison. She ordered Lü Chan, the king of Lu, to take over the southern garrison. "When Emperor Gaozu conquered the empire," she warned them, "he made an agreement with his followers that if anyone not of the Liu family became a king, the empire should join together in attacking him. Now the members of the Lü family have become kings, and the great ministers are displeased. The emperor is very young, and I fear that when I die, the ministers will make trouble for you. You must bring your soldiers over to guard the palace. Take care not to accompany the funeral procession. Do not allow yourselves to be coerced by others!"

Empress Lü died [in 180 BCE]. In her will, she left fifty-five pounds of gold to each of the kings who had been advanced from the rank of noble, as well as grants of gold to the generals, ministers, nobles, and palace officials according to their ranks, and she issued a general pardon all across the empire. She appointed Lü Chan, the king of Lu, as prime minister, and she made the daughter of Lü Lu the empress to the boy ruler.

[The remainder of the chapter tells the story of the violent suppression of the Lü family.]

The Grand Astrologer comments: During the time of Emperor Hui the Loyal Son and Empress Lü, the black-headed people left behind the sufferings of the period of the Warring States,[6] and all the subordinate lords and vassals observed nonaction as their governing policy. Emperor Hui therefore let his sleeves fall and folded his arms in front of him. Empress Lü, as a woman ruler, proclaimed that she would issue imperial decrees and arranged to rule without leaving her rooms in the palace. The world was at peace, punishments and penalties were rarely imposed, and criminals became few. The people devoted themselves to planting and harvesting, and clothing and food became more and more plentiful.

---

[6]The period from 476 BCE to the unification of China by the First Emperor of Qin in 221 BCE.

11

Heroic Hermits: The Biographies of Bo Yi and Shu Qi

This excerpt comes from the first chapter of "Biographies," which constitutes the largest part of The Records of the Historian. *It is one of the best-known stories from Chinese history, famous for its implications concerning the nature of power, honor, genuine success and happiness, and divine justice. The story subtly poses the question of whether retirement from the world can be as noble as participating in it. The chapter's placement at the beginning of the biographical section (which contains seventy biographies) makes it an implicit introduction to other key themes in the section, such as the historian's purpose and responsibility in describing and analyzing the past, including the struggle to reconcile contradictory accounts and examine the relationship between human morality, fate, and the way of Heaven.*

Bo Yi and Shu Qi belonged to the legendary past, when the Zhou dynasty (ca. 1045–256 BCE) replaced the Shang dynasty.

[Sima Qian] says that scholars refer to a deep and wide range of books and records, and in addition they must cross-reference their sources' reliability with the *Six Classics*. Even though the *Classics of Poetry* and *Classic of Documents* are missing some sections, literary records of the Yu and Xia dynasties are still accessible. When Yao was about to yield his throne to Shun of the Yu dynasty, all the high-ranking officials suggested that both Shun of the Yu dynasty and Yu of the Xia dynasty be given a trial period of several decades in this position. When their abilities proved to be worthy, they then officially held power, one after the other. This shows that the world is an important crucible, that its rulers form a tradition, and that their line of succession is full of difficulties.

Furthermore, some say that Yao yielded the kingship to Xü You, but the latter would not take it. Thinking this was a shameful situation, he hid himself away as a hermit. Further, at the time of the

From Sima Qian, *The Records of the Historian*, chap. 61.

Xia dynasty, there were Bian Sui and Wu Guang.[1] Why are their stories not told? The Grand Astrologer reports, "When I climbed Mount Ji, I found the tomb of Xü You on the summit as proof of his historical reality. Confucius listed the ancient sages, men of wisdom and excellence, and mentioned in detail such figures as Tai Bo of the kingdom of Wu and Bo Yi. I am told that Xü You and Wu Guang were men of the highest excellence, and yet in the Confucian texts these men were not mentioned. Why not?"

Confucius said, "Bo Yi and Shu Qi did not remember wrongs done to them and in general resented no one. Since their searches for kindness were met with kindness, what reason would they have for resentment?" The Grand Astrologer says, "I feel sad about Bo Yi's purpose, but when I read his poem, I find it strange. Their biographies go as follows":

Bo Yi and Shu Qi were two of the sons of the ruler of Guzhu. The ruler himself wanted to designate Shu Qi, a younger son, as his heir. But when the father died, Shu Qi yielded the throne to his eldest brother, Bo Yi. Bo Yi said that they must obey their father's wish, and he ran off. Shu Qi did not want to become the ruler, and so he ran off as well. The people of the nation installed the middle son as ruler instead. By this time, Bo Yi and Shu Qi, having heard that Chang, earl of the west, took good care of the elderly, both wanted to go live with him. But by the time they arrived, Chang had died. His son King Wu was carrying around with him the spiritual tablet of his dead father[2] [instead of installing it in the ancestral shrine]. He honored his father with the title "King Wen." He then marched east to attack Zhou, the emperor of Shang.

Bo Yi and Shu Qi, clutching the reins of King Wu's horse, reprimanded him by saying, "Your late father still lies unburied, and yet you have taken up arms to make war. Can a faithful son behave this way? When you, a subject, try to kill your emperor, are you behaving kindly?" The attendants of King Wu wanted to have the soldiers kill Bo Yi and Shu Qi, but his counselor said, "These are two men of justice," and he helped them go free.

After King Wu put down the uprising of Yin, the whole world accepted the Zhou dynasty, except for Bo Yi and Shu Qi. They

---

[1]These are legendary figures from the Shang dynasty, who also refused to accept rule when it was offered to them.

[2]This was a marker identifying the dead person that was used in the rituals of ancestor worship.

regarded it as shameful. Their desire to behave correctly led them to refuse to eat the grain of Zhou. They went to live as hermits on Shouyang Mountain, where they gathered ferns as their food until they starved to death. They left behind a song: "We climbed up this West Mountain, alas, and picked its ferns. We don't know, alas, whether it is right or wrong to exchange violence for violence. Since Shen Nong, Yu, and Xia[3] all, alas, disappeared suddenly, how can we find our way home and rest? Our fate, alas, has gone wrong." They starved to death on Shouyang Mountain.

[The Grand Astrologer] says, "When we view the matter from this angle, should we believe that there was resentment or not?

"Some say that Heaven favors no one automatically, as if a family member, but does favor the morally good. Can such men as Bo Yi and Shu Qi be called morally good or not? Although Confucius singled out Yan Yuen from his seventy disciples for his love of learning, nevertheless Yan Yuen never received even enough poor food and in the end died young. How can this be Heaven's way to reward the morally good?

"Zhi, the bandit, killed innocent people every day, ate their flesh, and acted cruelly and violently, ganging up with thousands to commit crimes across the world. And yet he lived to a very old age. What moral standards was he following to achieve this?

"These are the best-known examples. In recent years, people's conduct has become even more unruly. They willfully do unspeakable things and take forbidden actions, but they remain carefree and happy all their lives and wealthy for generations on end.

"Men who choose carefully where to proceed, wait patiently for the right moment to offer their advice, take no shortcuts, and never vent their pent-up emotions, unless it is for what is right and fair, nevertheless meet with countless disasters and catastrophes. I am deeply perplexed by their afflictions. Is the so-called Way of Heaven meant to be like that, or is it not?

"Confucius said that those who walk on different paths cannot meet to consult with each other. This means that each one follows his own intentions. Thus he said, 'If there was a way to get wealth and rank, even serving as a lowly whip holder, I would take it. If not, I would just follow my own desires.' Only when the season turns cold does one know that pines and cedars are the last to lose their leaves. When the whole world is muddy, the pure man emerges. Why in the world is something heavy like that, but something else is light like this?

[3]These are legendary founders of early Chinese civilization.

"A superior man hates to leave the world without being remembered with praise." Master Jia Yi said that the greedy man dies for wealth, the martyr dies for fame, and the boaster dies for power. The common man clings to life. Lights of the same brightness reflect each other, and lights of the same kind seek each other. Clouds follow the dragon, and winds follow the tiger. When the sages act, all creatures can see them. Bo Yi and Shu Qi, though morally good by themselves, had their fame increase when Confucius discussed them. Although Yan Yuen was diligent in learning, his taking hold of the horse's tail[4] made his achievements more notable. The hermit scholars may be ever so correct in their timing of when to give and when to accept, but their names and their kind are lost and forgotten without a word of praise. What a pity! Men of humble origins strive to perfect their actions to establish a name for themselves. But if they do not attach themselves to a pure man of high rank, how can even a little be passed down to future generations?

[4]That is, Confucius.

12

Arts of War: The Biographies of Sun Wu and Sun Bin

This excerpt presents two of the three stories about military experts from chapter 65 of the "Biographies" section. Sun Wu (or Sunzi Wu), who lived in the late sixth/early fifth centuries BCE, is famous today as the author of the handbook The Art of War, *which advocates ruthlessness and deception in waging war. Sun Bin also wrote a book on the same topic. Their advocacy of this approach to war disturbed those who followed Confucian principles, which were seen as promoting more humane and straightforward tactics. This document therefore provides material for thinking about whether the same standard of justice applies in the conduct of warfare as in everyday life. It also addresses women's capacity for war as compared to men's.*

From Sima Qian, *The Records of the Historian*, chap. 65.

Sun Wu, a native of Qi, was granted an audience by King He Lu of Wu [r. 514–496 BCE], so that he could present his book on the art of war to the king. He Lu said, "I have read all your thirteen chapters. Now can you try to train a few troops for me?" He replied, "I certainly can!" He Lu said, "Could you try with women as well?" He replied, "I certainly can!" So he was given permission to proceed.

One hundred eighty beautiful women from the king's palace were made available. Sun Wu divided them into two troops and made the king's two favorite concubines the troop leaders. He had them all hold halberds.[1] He gave them orders, asking, "Do you know front from back, left from right?" The women said, "We do." Sun Wu told them, "When you are ordered to go forward, you go straight, looking in the direction of your chest; to go left, look toward your left hand; to go right, look toward your right hand; to retreat, turn backward." The women said, "All right!"

Having laid down these rules, he made swords and axes ready and repeated his instructions over and over again. Then he had drums beaten as a signal and gave the order to turn right. The women burst out laughing. Sun Wu said, "If the rules are unclear and the commands are unfamiliar, the commander is to blame." He repeated his instructions. Then he beat the drums and gave the order for a left turn. But once more the women burst into laughter. Sun Wu said, "If the rules are unclear and the commands are unfamiliar, the commander is to blame, but when orders are fully understood and yet not carried out, it should be the officers who are to blame." So he wanted to behead both troop leaders.

The king of Wu, watching from his observation terrace, saw that his favorite concubines were to be executed momentarily. He was in shock. He quickly sent one of his messengers to pass on his order to Sun Wu, saying, "I have been completely convinced that you are a well-qualified commander of troops. However, without those two beloved concubines of mine in my future, my food is going to become tasteless! I would much rather you not behead them." Sun Wu said, "Your servant has received his appointment to be the commander. 'When a commander is in his camp, there will be orders from his ruler that he need not accept.'"[2] He then beheaded both of the troop leaders as an example [to the other women]. He made the next women in line the troop leaders and beat the drum once more. This time the women

---

[1]Long weapons combining a battle-ax and a pike.
[2]This is a quotation from *The Art of War*.

went left, right, forward, backward, knelt down, and rose up, all done exactly as commanded, as if being directed by an inked rope.[3] They dared not speak a single word.

Then Sun Wu sent a messenger to the king, reporting, "The soldiers are ready for action. Your Majesty is welcome to come out anytime for inspection and to use them any way that you wish. Even if you send them through fire and water, they are ready to serve." The king of Wu said, "Retire to your dwelling, General. I have no more desire to go down there to watch this." Sun Wu remarked, "Your Majesty only wants to have an army in name, but not in reality." From then on, He Lu realized that Sun Wu was truly talented and skilled in military affairs, and eventually he made him his commander. They defeated mighty Chu on the western border, entering that state's capital, Ying, and in the north they struck awe into Qi and Jin. Their fame spread among the subordinate lords, mainly due to Sun Wu's efforts.

Sun Bin lived more than a hundred years after the death of Sun Wu. Bin was born in the area of Ngo and Juan. Bin was a descendant of Sun Wu. Sun Bin once studied the art of war together with Pang Juan. Pang Juan later served in Wei and became King Huei's general. Being aware that he was not as skilled a warrior as Sun Bin, Pang Juan sent a secret messenger to have Sun Bin come to him. After Sun Bin arrived, Pang Juan became jealous of him, fearing that he might become more honored than himself. So he framed him on a legal charge, causing him to be punished by having both his feet amputated and his face tattooed. He hoped that Sun Bin would hide from public view from then on.

When a messenger from Qi came to Liang, the capital of Wei, Sun Bin, since he was a convict who had suffered mutilation, had to meet him secretly to offer his advice. He impressed the messenger greatly, who was surprised at what he found. So he smuggled Bin out of the region of Wei in his carriage and took him back to Qi. The general of Qi, Tian Ji, welcomed him with courtesy and took him in as his guest. Tian Ji raced horses and often gambled heavily with Qi's nobles. Sun Bin noticed that the speed of the horses did not differ much but that all the horses could be divided into high, middle, and low grades. So he said to Tian Ji, "Just bet heavily, my lord, and I can make you the winner." Tian Ji trustingly agreed and bet one thousand pieces of gold on a race pitting his horses against those owned by the king and the

---

[3]That is, as if they were following the straight lines marked by a carpenter while doing construction work.

noblemen of Qi. Just before the bet was made, Sun Bin said, "Now match your low-grade horses with their high-grade horses, your high-grade horses with their middle-grade horses, and your middle-grade horses with their low-grade horses." After they raced the three grades in three races, Tian Ji lost once but won twice, and in the end he won the thousand pieces of gold from the king. After that, Tian Ji presented Sun Bin to King Wei of Qi. The king questioned him on the art of war and then appointed him as his adviser.

After a while, Wei attacked Zhao, and in desperation Zhao turned to Qi for help. King Wei of Qi wanted his army to be commanded by Sun Bin, but Bin declined, saying, "Not by a mutilated man." So Tian Ji was made the commander and Sun Bin his adviser. Sun Bin sat in a covered wagon and drew up plans and strategies. Tian Ji wanted to lead his troops to Zhao, but Sun Bin advised him, "To unravel a messy fight, one does not use a fist; to settle a dispute, one does not use a weapon of assassination. Arrange your defenses well and attack their weak points. In this way, further entanglements become impossible, and things will resolve themselves. Now that Liang and Zhao are at war, their light-armed soldiers and elite troops are sure to have all been sent to battle far away, leaving none but the old and disabled ones at home. Why don't you immediately lead your army to Liang, occupy its streets and roads, and attack while it is undefended? The enemy will then leave Zhao alone and rush back home to save itself. We will in one swoop lift the siege of Zhao and exhaust Wei's force." Tian Ji acted on his advice, and Wei indeed left Handan, fought with Qi at Guiling, and was soundly defeated.

Thirteen years later, Wei and Zhao attacked Han together, and Han asked Qi for help. Qi dispatched Tian Ji as general, and he marched straight to Liang. When the Wei general Pang Juan heard of this, he returned from Han, but by then the forces of Qi had advanced farther west. At this point, Sun Bin advised Tian Ji, "The soldiers of Wei have always been brave and strong and have shown contempt for the men of Qi, giving them the name cowards. A skilled general makes use of the situation and leads efficiently. According to *The Art of War*, 'When an army hurries to advance for twenty-four miles, the commander might die; when it hurries to advance for twelve miles, only half the force arrives.' When Qi's army enters Wei territory, first light a hundred thousand cooking fires. The next day, light only fifty thousand, and the day after, light fires for only thirty thousand." On the third day of Pang Juan's march, he was overjoyed and said, "I always knew Qi's troops were cowards. Three days in our territory, and more than half of their officers and their men have deserted."

Leaving his infantry behind, Pang Juan took with him only light cavalry so he could press on at twice the pace in hot pursuit. Sun Bin calculated that the pursuers would reach Maling by evening. The road in Maling was narrow, with lots of obstacles on both sides where ambushes could be prepared. He stripped the bark off a large tree and wrote on the trunk, "Pang Juan dies under this tree!" Then he ordered ten thousand expert archers to hide on both sides of the road and wait for the signal. "As soon as you see a flame lit after sunset, all of you shoot at the same time." When Pang Juan came to the stripped tree and saw the writing, he ordered a light to read it. Before he could finish reading, the ten thousand bowmen of the Qi army discharged their arrows, and the Wei army was thrown into chaotic confusion. Pang Juan realized that he had been outwitted and his troops defeated. He then cut his throat, saying, "So I have helped this wretch make a name for himself!" Qi, with its great success, completely defeated Wei's army and captured Shen, the prince of Wei, before returning home. Sun Bin's name became famous everywhere. His *Art of War* was handed down to later generations. . . .

The Grand Astrologer comments: . . . Many people today have these men's writings, so I have not included those works but rather the men's actions and achievements. There is a saying, "Those who are able to do something are not always able to talk about it, and those who can talk about something are not always able to do it." Sun Bin devised an ingenious strategy against Pang Juan, but previously he was not able to prevent himself from being horribly mutilated.

13

Imperial Assassin: The Biography of Jing Ke

This selection comes from a "Biographies" chapter narrating the stories of five assassins and retainers (subordinates pledged to be loyal to their superior). The stories focus on violent actions, but they also include themes relevant to defining loyalty, especially that owed by an inferior to a superior. They became very famous, and later Chinese poets, playwrights, and authors often used them as inspiration. The historian Ban Gu, however, criticized Sima Qian for glamorizing murderous thugs. His criticism seems remarkably like modern condemnations of the portrayal of violence in the media as inciting brutality in viewers. It seems worth considering whether historians are responsible for the reactions that their works might trigger in their audiences.

Jing Ke's attempt to murder the man who would become the First Emperor of Qin (r. 221–210 BCE) took place in 227 BCE.

Jing Ke came from Wei. His ancestors came from Qi but migrated to Wei. . . . He liked reading and swordsmanship. He tried to impress the ruler of Wei, Prince Yuan, with his knowledge of swordplay, but the prince did not hire him. . . . Jing Ke once visited Yuci during his travels, where he discussed swordsmanship with Gai Nie. Gai Nie became angry and glared at him. When Jing Ke walked out, someone suggested they should call him back. Gai Nie said, "Whenever in the past I would discuss swordsmanship with anyone, if I didn't think he made sense, I would glare at him. It is perfectly all right to try to find him, but he should have left. I am sure he would not have dared to stay." A messenger was sent to the traveler's host, but Jing Ke had already harnessed his horse and left Yuci. When the messenger returned with this news, Gai Nie said, "He had a reason to go; I stared that guy down."

Jing Ke traveled to Handan and gambled with Lu Goujian. When they had a dispute, Lu Goujian became angry and shouted at him. Jing Ke immediately left without saying good-bye. They never met again. Having reached the state of Yan, Jing Ke made friends with a butcher who specialized in selling dog meat and the lute player Gao Jianli. Jing Ke liked wine very much, and he spent his days drinking in the

---

From Sima Qian, *The Records of the Historian,* chap. 86.

marketplace of the Yan capital with the dog butcher and Gao Jianli. When they got drunk, Gao Jianli played the lute and Jing Ke sang with him in the marketplace. They were merry together, but they could also weep together, as if no one else was around. Jing Ke was certainly a heavy drinker, but he was habitually serious, stern, profound, and studious. He made friends with people of quality, wealth, and respect in all the states of the subordinate lords he visited. In the state of Yan, the retired scholar Tian Guang received him kindly, recognizing that he was no ordinary man.

A bit later, Prince Dan of Yan escaped from Qin, where he had been held as a diplomatic hostage, and returned home. Prince Dan had once been held as a diplomatic hostage in Zhao. King Zheng of Qin was born in Zhao, where they were playmates together and got along very well. When Zheng became king of Qin, Dan was a diplomatic hostage in Qin. But the king of Qin treated the prince badly, so Dan fled home in resentment. After his return home, he looked for a way to even the score with the king of Qin, but his state was small and his strength insufficient.

After this, Qin sent troops daily to the east of the mountains, attacking Qi, Chu, and the three states of Jin, gradually nibbling away at the subordinate lords, until its army was close to reaching Yan. The king of Yan and his subordinate lords feared that a disaster loomed. Prince Dan was troubled and sought advice from his tutor, Ju Wu, who answered, "Qin possesses the whole world and now threatens the clans of Han, Wei, and Zhao. . . . Its population is large, its soldiers are well trained, and it has more than enough weapons for its troops. If Qin wants to proceed, there are still the areas south of the Great Wall and north of the Yi River left to conquer. So why risk rubbing its dragon scales the wrong way, just because you harbor resentment over being humiliated?" Prince Dan asked, "Then what other way is there?" "Let me sleep on it," Ju Wu replied.

Some time later, the Qin general Fan Yuqi offended his king and fled to Yan. The prince took him in and let him stay in his guesthouse. Ju Wu warned, "Please don't do this! The king of Qin is such a tyrant that his accumulated anger against Yan is enough to put fear into our hearts. It would be even worse if he hears that General Fan is taking refuge here. This amounts to throwing meat in the hungry tiger's way. Such a disaster would be beyond remedy! Not even Guan or Yan could devise any strategy to help you.[1] I beg you, my prince, please silence

---

[1] These were famous generals from an earlier time. Sima Qian describes their careers in chapter 62 of his work.

General Fan by immediately sending him in secret to the Xiongnu [see Document 14], then make an alliance with the three states of Jin in the west, join with Qi and Chu in the south, and come to terms with the Xiongnu's chief in the north. Then we can form a plan."

The prince said, "The Grand Tutor's plan is too time-consuming, and I am too impatient to wait for even one more moment. Not only that, General Fan has now come to me for protection, and I must not let Qin's strength intimidate me into discarding such a friend with whom I sympathize. To send him to the Xiongnu—why, I would much rather die than do that. I wish the Grand Tutor would reconsider this plan." Ju Wu said, "If one follows a dangerous path to win safety, this is risking disaster to gain good fortune and making a shortsighted plan that will create long-lasting resentment. If one shows concern for a recent friendship with a man but disregards the great damage to the state, this is surely called feeding resentment and aiding disaster. If you place a swan feather on a stove of burning charcoal, it will soon disappear. And when Qin strikes like a vulture in all its fury, you do not need me to tell you how to go on! There is a scholar Tian Guang in our state who has great wisdom and moral courage. You might consult him."

The prince said, "I hope to meet the scholar Tian Guang through the Grand Tutor's introduction. Is it possible?" Ju Wu said, "I shall respectfully comply." Then he went to see Tian and said, "The prince wants to consult with you on affairs of state, sir." Tian Guang said, "I respectfully accept his instructions," and he went to see the prince.

Prince Dan welcomed him with great respect. He walked backward to lead him in, then knelt to dust off the seat for him. As soon as Tian Guang was seated and they were alone, the prince left his seat, rose to his feet, and pleaded, "Yan and Qin cannot exist together. Please consider this situation, sir," he said. Tian Guang said, "I, your servant, have heard that a good stallion in its prime can gallop 250 miles in a day, but when it grows old, the poorest nag can overtake it. The Prince has heard of me in my prime, but he does not realize that my strength is gone. Although this is true and therefore I would not dare to allow you to consult me on affairs of state, yet Jing, whom I know well, can be trusted to take care of this matter." The prince said, "I hope to make friends with Jing through you, sir. Is this possible?" Tian Guang said, "I shall respectfully comply." He rose immediately and hurried out. The prince escorted him to the door and warned, "What I have reported to you and what you have spoken about to me are crucial affairs of state, sir. I beg you not to let it leak out! Tian Guang laughed apologetically, saying, "Surely."

Stooping with age, Tian Guang went to see Jing and said, "You and I are good friends, as everybody in the state of Yan knows. Having heard of me in my prime, the prince does not realize my body is failing. He favored me with this instruction: 'Yan and Qin cannot coexist; please consider this situation.' Not wanting to pass the task on to some outsider, I told the prince about you, my close friend. I hope that you, my close friend, might go to see the prince at his palace." Jing Ke said, "Your instructions are sincerely accepted." Tian Guang said, "I have heard that actions of superior men do not cause others to suspect them. Now the prince told me, 'What we have spoken about are crucial affairs of the state; I beg you not to let it leak out!' Therefore, the prince suspects me. Those whose actions cause others to become suspicious are not just and responsible men of action." Tian Guang decided to commit suicide to provoke Jing Ke to take action, saying, "I hope that you, my close friend, will hurry to bring this message to the prince to inform him that Tian Guang has died to ensure his silence." He then cut his own throat and died.

Jing Ke met with the prince, told him that Tian Guang had died, and repeated Tian Guang's words. The prince bowed twice and knelt, crawled forward on his knees, and wept heavy tears. After quite a while, he sobbed, "The reason I warned Tian Guang not to speak was because I hoped that our crucial plan might succeed. Now Tian Guang has guaranteed his silence with death. This was never my intention!" Jing Ke sat down, and the prince left his seat, knocking his forehead against the ground and saying, "Since Tian Guang did not know my lack of worth, his daring provided the way for us to meet and speak. Evidently, Heaven has taken pity on Yan and does not abandon its orphan. Now Qin is greedy for profit, and its desires can never be satisfied. Not until it has conquered all the lands of the world and defeated all the kings will it be content. Qin has now captured the king of Han and seized all his land. Its troops attacked Chu in the south and confronted Zhao in the north. . . . Zhao cannot resist Qin and must surrender, and then it will be Yan's turn. Yan is small and weak, exhausted by continuous warfare. Even if we mobilize the entire country, we cannot repel Qin's invasion. Moreover, the other states are too submissive to Qin to attempt an alliance against a common enemy.

"My humble plan is for us to obtain the world's bravest man to be our messenger to Qin. He will tempt its king with a large profit, and the greedy king of Qin is surely going to want to take it. It will be ideal if, by doing this, we can kidnap the king of Qin and make him return all the lands he seized from the subordinate lords, in the same way that Cao Mo did with Qi Huangong.[2] If not, the messenger can then stab him to death. Then, with generals commanding armies outside their borders and with trouble at home, the king and his subordinate lords will suspect each other, allowing the subordinates to conspire against him. The destruction of Qin will be assured. Such is my great expectation, but I do not know to whom I might entrust the mission. Only you are able to consider the matter."

After a long while, Jing Ke said, "This is a crucial matter of state. I am too inferior to carry it out." The prince proceeded to knock his forehead on the ground to beg him not to refuse, and in the end Jing Ke agreed. Thus Jing Ke was made a senior noble and housed in a fine mansion. The prince visited him daily and supplied him with the finest of delicacies. He presented him with precious gifts, carriages, and beautiful girls to satisfy Jing Ke's every whim and fancy.

This went on for a long time, and Jing Ke made no move to proceed. General Wang Jin of Qin defeated Zhao, captured its king, annexed the whole state, and advanced northward to occupy all the areas up to the southern boundary of Yan. Prince Dan was desperate, and he begged Jing Ke, "The army of Qin may cross the Yi River any moment now. Then I will no longer be able to entertain you, much as I would like to!" Jing Ke said, "The Prince needs to say nothing. I, your servant, was going to try to see you to talk about the situation. Now, if I go without some proof to gain the confidence of Qin, I may not be welcomed. The king of Qin has offered a thousand pieces of gold and rule over ten thousand households as a reward for General Fan. If I could get the head of General Fan and a map of the Dukang district of Yan to present to the king of Qin, he would be pleased to see me, and I would be able to carry out your scheme." The prince said, "General Fan, poor and in need, came to me to take refuge. I could not betray an honorable man's trust for the sake of my own desires. I want you to rethink the matter."

Jing Ke knew that the prince was softhearted, so he went secretly to see Fan Yuqi and said, "General, Qin has treated you harshly indeed, and your parents and family members have all been killed. Now I hear that a thousand pieces of gold and rule over ten thousand households are offered for your head. Do you have any idea what to do?" Fan Yuqi looked up to heaven, breathed a great sigh, and said tearfully, "Whenever I think of this, I feel a deep pain in my bones, so

---

[2]This refers to the story that Sima Qian tells at the beginning of this chapter (not included here) of an assassin who forced a ruler to give up conquered territory.

deep that I don't know what to do!" Jing Ke said, "If one word can solve the trouble of the state of Yan and avenge the wrong you have suffered—what would you think of that?" Fan Yuqi said, "Tell me what to do." Jing Ke said, "If I could have your head to present to the king of Qin, he would be happy to see me. Then I will grab his sleeve with my left hand and stab him in the chest with my right hand. In this way, you will have revenge, and the prince's humiliation will be erased. Do you have the determination, General?" Fan Yuqi bared his shoulder, gripped his wrist, stepped forward, and said, "Day and night I ground my teeth and burned my heart waiting for this idea; you have now told me what to do!" He then killed himself. When the prince learned this, he hurried there to cry bitterly over the corpse. Then, since there was nothing else to do, the prince had Fan Yuqi's head placed in a sealed box.

Earlier, the prince had ordered a search for the sharpest dagger, and he had bought one from a man of Zhao by the name of Xu Furen for one hundred pieces of gold. Then he commanded his workers to put poison on the blade and experiment on people. Although the thrust drew barely enough blood to stain the robes of the victims, every one of them died while still standing. The dagger was therefore packed in Jing's baggage for his mission. There was a bold youngster of Yan named Qin Wuyang, who had begun his career as a killer at age thirteen. No one dared to look him in the eye. He was chosen to be Jing Ke's assistant. Jing Ke was waiting for another assistant of his own choice, but the man lived far away. To arrange to get this man, Jing Ke delayed his departure. The delay upset the prince, who suspected that Jing Ke had gone back on his promise. He said, "The day is getting short. Do you intend to start now? Or do you allow me to send Qin Wuyang on ahead?" Jing Ke angrily shouted at the prince, "What is it that the Prince is sending? To send that little boy by himself, you can be sure he will never return and that his mission will fail! What else is there to expect if one sets off with a single dagger to face the immeasurable power of Qin? The reason that I have delayed is that I was waiting for a friend to go with me. But if the Prince is upset by my delay, I beg you to let me take off right this minute!" Then off he went. . . .

When they arrived in Qin, Jing Ke presented gifts worth a thousand pieces of gold to Meng Jia, a palace counselor who was also a favorite subordinate of the king of Qin. Meng Jia then spoke on Jing Ke's behalf to the king, saying, "The king of Yan, shivering before Your Majesty, dares not raise troops to oppose your armies. He offers to submit to Qin, making himself one of your subordinate lords on regular terms, paying taxes and providing labor, as do your military regions and districts. He is willing to do these things so he can continue to sacrifice at the temple of his ancestors. In his fear, he dares not come in person to speak, but he has in respect cut off Fan Yuqi's head, and with it he presents a map of the Dukang region of Yan, sealed in boxes. The king of Yan bowed in sending these off to you from his court, instructing his messenger to bring all this to Your Majesty and await your orders."

This report greatly pleased the king of Qin, and he put on his formal robe and had nine levels of officials arrayed to receive the messenger of Yan in the Xianyang palace. Walking forward one behind the other, Jing Ke held aloft the box with Fan Yuqi's head, while Qin Wuyang carried the box with the map. When they reached the steps of the throne, Qin Wuyang turned pale and began to shake, which surprised the assembled ministers of the king. Jing Ke looked at Qin Wuyang and smiled, then stepped forward to apologize. "This country boy from the barbaric tribes of the north has never seen the Son of Heaven. That's why he is shaking. I beg the great king to pardon him a little so that he can complete his duties in your presence." The king of Qin said to Jing Ke, "Get me the map he is carrying." When Jing Ke took the map and presented it, the king unrolled the map, and at the end [of the scroll] the dagger appeared. Jing Ke grabbed the king's sleeve with his left hand, and with his right hand he picked up the dagger to stab at the king's chest. This startled the king, who jumped to his feet, which tore off his sleeve before the dagger reached his body. The king tried to draw his sword, but it was long and got stuck in its scabbard. He panicked, but the sword was completely stuck and could not be drawn. Jing Ke chased the king, who ran behind a column. The assembled ministers were all shocked, since this was so totally unexpected. They were thrown into a sudden and utter confusion.

Following Qin law, none of the king's ministers with him in the upper hall of the palace were permitted to carry even the smallest weapon. All the armed palace attendants were stationed below the hall, and they could not come up there without an order from the king. In his moment of panic, the king had no time to give that order, and Jing Ke was able to chase him. In their haste and fear, the king's ministers had nothing to fight Jing Ke with, so they together began hitting him with their bare hands. At this point, the king's doctor, Xia Wuzhu, threw his bag of medicine at Jing Ke. The king had just gone around the column, and in his desperation he did not know what to do. His ministers yelled, "The king should pull out his sword from behind him!" Putting the sword behind him, he pulled it out and struck Jing Ke, cutting him on his left thigh. Crippled by the wound, Jing Ke hurled his dagger at the king of Qin. He missed, hitting the column instead. The king of Qin attacked Jing Ke, wounding him eight more times. Knowing his attempt had failed, Jing Ke leaned against a column and laughed. As he collapsed, he cursed, "The reason my attempt failed is because, instead of assassinating you, I tried to forge an agreement that I could take back to Prince Dan of Yan!" At this, the king's ministers came forward and killed Jing Ke. The king remained disturbed for a long time. When he later evaluated his ministers for reward and punishment, he decided that everyone present was at fault in some way. He rewarded only Xia Wuzhu with two hundred pieces of gold, saying, "Because Wuzhu loves me, he threw his bag of medicine at Jing Ke."

Following this, the king of Qin became enraged and sent more troops to Zhao, ordering Wang Jian's army to besiege Yan. By the tenth month, the city of Zhicheng was taken. Xi, the king of Yan, and Dan, his heir, led their finest troops east to take refuge in Liaodong. Qin's general, Li Xin, pursued and fiercely attacked the king of Yan. Jia, the king of Dai, wrote to King Xi of Yan, saying, "Qin is pressing you so hard because of Prince Dan. If you present the head of Dan to the king of Qin, he will surely leave you alone, and your ancestral altar will be fortunate to receive its blood sacrifices." After that, Li Xin continued to pursue Dan, who concealed himself in the middle of the Yan River. The king of Yan sent a messenger to cut off Prince Dan's head, intending to present it to Qin, but Qin continued to attack. Five years later [222 BCE], Qin annexed Yan and captured King Xi of Yan.

The next year [221 BCE], Qin conquered the world, and the king took the title "emperor." Now Qin pursued the retainers of Prince Dan and Jing Ke. They all disappeared. Gao Jianli changed his name and became a bartender, hiding in Songzhi. After a while, he became sick and tired of his work, and whenever he heard a guest play the lute, he would hang around, unable to leave, mumbling under his breath, "He plays this part well but that part badly." The workers told their employer that the bartender understood and could evaluate music. So the woman of the house had him play the lute for the guests. Everyone said he played very well, and he was given wine. Thinking of his long period of hiding and of the endless hardship ahead, Gao Jianli excused himself to take his lute from his luggage and change to better clothing, so that he could improve his image. Everyone there was surprised, and they greeted him with respect, treating him as an honored guest. Whenever he was asked to play the lute and sing, the audience was always moved to tears. The people of Songzhi took turns having him as a guest. The First Emperor of Qin heard about this and wanted to see him. Someone then recognized him and said, "This is Gao Jianli," but the emperor liked his lute playing and granted him a pardon. However, he put out his eyes. Whenever the emperor commanded him to play, he always earned praise. The emperor sat closer and closer to him to listen. Gao Jianli put a piece of heavy lead in his lute. When he again came to court and got closer to the emperor, Gao Jianli lifted his lute and hurled it at the emperor, but he missed. So Gao Jianli was executed. For the rest of his life, the emperor never allowed men of the subordinate states to come near him.

When Lu Goujian heard of Jing Ke's attempt to assassinate the king of Qin, he said privately, "What a pity! He did not study carefully the way to do an assassination using a sword! How mistaken I was in judging him! I yelled at him once, and he must have thought that I was not a man worth any consideration!"

The Grand Astrologer comments: "When people of our time talk about Jing Ke, they assert that what happened to Prince Dan was 'heaven raining grain and horses sprouting horns.' This is too much! They also claim that Jing Ke wounded the king of Qin, which is not true. . . . Of the five assassins and retainers [whose stories appear in the complete version of this chapter of Sima Qian's work], some succeeded and some failed in their missions of justice. Nevertheless, it is completely obvious that they all had determination in fulfilling their tasks. They did not shortchange their goals. How can it be wrong that their names are passed down to be known by subsequent generations?"

14

How Others Live: The Customs of the Xiongnu

The people whom the Chinese called the Xiongnu (fierce slaves), regarding them as uncivilized barbarians, were a group of nomadic tribes inhabiting what are today the plains of Mongolia, north of China. The Xiongnu existed on the border of China from an early date, though Sima Qian is describing them here as they were in the period preceding — and into — his lifetime. Xiongnu warriors were famous for their accuracy in shooting their bows while riding full speed on horseback, and they periodically launched violent raids into China. Notice how Sima Qian's description of their history and customs illuminates Chinese attitudes about civilized behavior, courage and virtue, and the proper role model for political rule. On this last topic, it is worth comparing what the Chinese eunuch Zhonghang Yue says to the Xiongnu in this selection with what Cyrus says to the Persians at the end of Document 6.

The ancestor of the Xiongnu descended from the ruler of the Xia dynasty, whose name was Qun Wei. From before the time of Emperors Yao and Shun [third millennium BCE], there have been barbarians... living in northern uncivilized areas and wandering around herding animals. They herd mainly horses, cattle, and sheep, but also some unusual animals, such as camels, donkeys, mules, and wild horses.... They move around looking for water and pasture and have no walled settlements or permanent housing. They do not farm, but they do divide their land into separate holdings under different leaders. They have no writing, and all contracts are verbal. When their children can ride a sheep, they begin to use bows and arrows to shoot birds and rodents. When they are older, they shoot foxes and rabbits for food. In this way, all the young men are easily able to become archers and serve as cavalry. It is their custom when times are easy to graze their animals and hunt with the bow for their living, but when hard times come, they take up weapons to plunder and raid. This is their innate nature. Their long-range weapons are bows and arrows; they use swords and spears in close combat. When they have the advantage in

From Sima Qian, *The Records of the Historian*, chap. 110.

battle, they advance, but if not, they retreat, since there is no shame in running away. They are only concerned with self-interest, knowing nothing of proper behavior or justice.

Everyone, including the chiefs, eats the meat of their domesticated animals and wears clothing of hides and coats of fur. The men who are in their prime eat the fattiest and best food, while the elderly eat what is left over, since the Xiongnu treasure the strong and healthy but place little value on the weak and old. When his father dies, a son marries his stepmother, and when brothers die, the surviving brothers marry their widows. They have personal names but no family names or additional names. . . .

[By 221 BCE] the state of Qin had finally defeated the other six states of China [to create a unified empire]. The First Emperor of Qin sent General Meng Tian with 100,000 men to attack the barbarians in the north. He won control of all the lands south of the Yellow River and made the river into a defended border. Meng Tian built forty-four walled settlements along the river and filled them with convicts sentenced to labor and sent to the border to do garrison duty. He also constructed the direct road from Jiuyuan to Yunyang. In this way, he used the slopes of the mountain and the valleys to create a defended border, erecting ramparts and fortifications at needed points. The entire line of defense stretched over two thousand miles from Lintao to Liaodong and even crossed the Yellow River, running through Yangshan and Beijia. . . .

The chief of the Xiongnu was named Touman. Too weak to resist the army of Qin, Touman had retreated to the far north, where he held out with his subjects for more than a decade. Following Meng Tian's death, the revolt of the subordinate lords against the Qin dynasty created conflict and unrest in China. The convict laborers that the Qin dynasty had sent to garrison the border seized this opportunity to return home. When the Xiongnu discovered that no one was defending the border, they crossed the Yellow River southward into their old territory and established themselves along China's previous border.

Touman's oldest son and heir apparent as chief of the Xiongnu was named Maodun, but Touman also had a younger son from a different mother whom he had married later. Touman loved this woman very much and decided to eliminate Maodun, to make the younger son his heir. Touman therefore sent Maodun as a diplomatic hostage held by the Yuezhi.[1] As soon as Maodun reached the Yuezhi, Touman suddenly attacked them. They were on the verge of executing Maodun in

---

[1] Barbarians living to the east.

revenge for the attack when he stole one of their best horses and got away. When he made his way home, his courage so impressed Touman that he made Maodun the commander of a cavalry unit of ten thousand men.

Maodun had arrows made that whistled in flight and trained his men to shoot their bows as they were riding. He ordered, "He who does not shoot where my whistling arrow hits will be executed!" He then went out hunting birds and animals, and if any of his men failed to shoot at what he shot at with his whistling arrow, he immediately beheaded them. Next, he shot a whistling arrow at his own favorite horse. Some of his men hesitated, not daring to shoot the horse. Maodun beheaded them. A little later, he used a whistling arrow to shoot at his favorite wife. Again, some of his men, perhaps because they were afraid, did not dare to shoot. Once more, Maodun beheaded them. Later, he went hunting with his men and shot his father's best horse. All his men shot it, too. Then Maodun knew that he could rely on his troops. Accompanying Touman on a hunting trip, he shot a whistling arrow at his father. All his followers shot where the whistling arrow struck and killed the chief. Next, Maodun murdered his stepmother, his younger brother, and all the senior officers who refused to follow his commands. So Maodun made himself the chief [in 209 BCE].

At the time when Maodun was installed as chief, the eastern barbarians were very strong. Learning that Maodun had murdered his father to make himself the chief, they sent a messenger to him to say that they wanted Touman's famous horse that could run 250 miles in a single day. Maodun discussed this with his subordinates, who all said, "The 250-mile horse is a treasure of the Xiongnu. Don't give it to them!" Maodun, however, remarked, "How can you get along with your neighbors if you covet the same horse?" So he gave them the 250-mile horse. A little later, the eastern barbarians, who imagined that Maodun feared them, sent a messenger asking for one of the chief's wives. Maodun again questioned his subordinates, who angrily answered, "The eastern barbarians have no sense of proper behavior, asking for one of the chief's wives! Please attack them!" Maodun said, "How can you get along with your neighbors if you covet the same woman?" He then sent his favorite wife to the eastern barbarians. This increased the arrogance of the eastern barbarian king, and he launched an invasion westward. There was an uninhabitable wasteland of more than 250 miles between his territory and that of the Xiongnu; the two peoples lived on the edges of this wasteland. The eastern barbarian king's messenger told Maodun, "The Xiongnu are unable to use this uninhabited land beyond their border, and we would like to take it." When Maodun consulted his subordinates, they said, "This is wasteland. Therefore, it is acceptable to give it to them, or not to give it to them." At this point, Maodun became enraged, saying, "Land is the core of a nation! How can I give it away?" He also executed all those who advised giving away the land.

He then mounted his horse and rode off to attack the eastern barbarians, sending commands throughout his land that he would execute anyone who delayed in following him. Since the eastern barbarians had at first looked down on Maodun, they did not prepare a defense against him. Therefore, when he arrived with his army and attacked, he completely destroyed them, killing the ruler of the eastern barbarians and capturing his people with their animals and property. He then turned west, scattering the Yuezhi and seizing the lands of the rulers of Loufan and Boyang, south of the Yellow River. In this way, he recovered all the lands that General Meng Tian of Qin had ripped away from the Xiongnu. His border and that of the Han Empire followed the original Yellow River defense line all the way to the Chaona and Fushi districts. Next, he invaded the lands of Yan and Dai. At this time, the Han military was in a stalemate with the armies of Xiang Yu, and China was worn-out by war. For this reason, Maodun was able to build up his strength, and he assembled 300,000 archers. From the time of Qun Wei to that of Maodun, more than a thousand years had passed. . . . The Xiongnu reached the height of their power under Maodun. They subjugated all the barbarians to the north and had only China to the south as a rival power. . . .

At the start of the year, their leaders hold a small gathering at the chief's location. By the fifth month, a large meeting takes place at Longcheng, during which they offer sacrifices to their ancestors, Heaven and Earth, and the gods and spirits. In the fall, when the horses are fat, they hold another large meeting in the Dai forest. There they count up the number of persons and animals. According to their law, anyone who pulls out his sword one foot from its scabbard receives the death penalty, while those convicted of theft have their property confiscated. They punish minor crimes by whipping and major ones by execution. Nobody is held in confinement for more than ten days, and no more than a handful of men are in jail in the entire nation. At dawn the chief rises to worship the sun as it rises, and at night he does the same to the moon. . . . When a ruler dies, his favorite ministers and concubines must follow him in death, and they often number in the hundreds or even thousands.

Whenever they start some action, they track the stars and the moon. They launch attacks at the full moon and pull back their army when the moon wanes. Following a battle, they award a jug of wine to those who have cut off the heads of enemies, and they are allowed to keep the plunder that they have seized. They make slaves of any prisoners of war. Therefore, when they make war, each warrior works for his own profit. They are very skilled at using decoy soldiers to trick opponents to their destruction. As soon as they see the enemy, they go after their booty like a flock of birds hungry for prey, but when they are defeated, they disperse and evaporate like mist. Anyone who brings back a fallen comrade's body from the battlefield is given all the dead man's property. . . .

At this time, the Han dynasty under Gaozu [r. 206–195 BCE] had just succeeded in winning control of the empire. . . . Emperor Gaozu personally commanded an army to confront the Xiongnu. It was winter, and there was such cold weather and heavy snow that frostbite took off the fingers of two or three out of every ten of his men. Maodun pretended to withdraw, to lure the Han soldiers into chasing him. When they did so, Maodun hid all his strongest troops, letting his weakest and smallest men be spotted. So the entire Han army, including 320,000 infantry, marched northward in fast pursuit.

Emperor Gaozu reached Pingcheng before his foot soldiers did. Maodun attacked with 400,000 of his best cavalry, encircling Emperor Gaozu on White Peak for a week. The trapped Han soldiers could not get supplies from their comrades outside. The Xiongnu cavalry rode white horses on the west side, dark horses on the east, black horses on the north, and brown horses on the south. But Emperor Gaozu secretly sent a messenger to Maodun's wife with expensive presents. She then said to Maodun, "Rulers of two nations should not make trouble for each other. Even if you occupy all the lands of the Han dynasty, you will not want to live there. What's more, the Han emperor also has divinities as his guardians. I beg you, Your Majesty, to look into this closely."

Maodun had arranged a meeting with the troops of Wang Huang and Zhao Li, two of King Xin's[2] generals, but they did not show up. He therefore suspected that they were conspiring with the Han force. So he decided to follow his wife's advice and withdraw his men from one part of the encirclement. Emperor Gaozu commanded his troops to

---

[2]Xin was a Chinese subordinate ruler during the Han dynasty, who had surrendered to the Xiongnu and was now cooperating with them against the emperor.

load their bows with arrows for a breakthrough and march through the gap to rejoin the main Han infantry force. Maodun then departed with his cavalry. The Han army withdrew, sending Liu Jing to conclude a peace treaty and marriage alliance with the Xiongnu.

After this, King Xin, serving as a general for the Xiongnu, together with his force including Zhao Li and Wang Huang, repeatedly broke the peace treaty by raiding Dai and Yunzhong. Soon after, Chen Xi[3] rebelled to join with King Xin in conspiring to attack Dai. Fan Kuai of Han was sent to fight them, and he succeeded in recovering the provinces and districts of Dai, Yanmen, and Yunzhong. He did not, however, advance past the border. At this time, many Han generals surrendered to the Xiongnu, so Maodun raided Dai over and over. For this reason, he was a constant irritant to the Han. Emperor Gaozu therefore sent Liu Jing to present a princess from the imperial household to Maodun as his wife, along with tribute[4] to be sent annually, consisting of set amounts of silk, cloth, wine, grain, and foods, so that the two nations could exist in peace and brotherhood. Thereafter, Maodun plundered the border region less often. Later, the king of Yan, Lu Wan, revolted and took several thousand followers with him across the border, to surrender to the Xiongnu. They roamed back and forth in Shang Gu and eastward, creating much turmoil.

Then Emperor Gaozu died. Emperor Hui and Empress Lü were just consolidating their power, and the Xiongnu became very arrogant. Maodun sent an insulting letter to Empress Lü. The empress wanted to send a military expedition against Maodun, but her generals told her, "Even Emperor Gaozu, with his wisdom and bravery, had great difficulty at Pingcheng." In the end, she gave up the idea of an attack and resumed friendly relations with the Xiongnu. . . .

When Maodun died [in 174 BCE], his son Jizhu became chief. Emperor Wen [r. 180–157 BCE] sent him a princess from the imperial household as a wife. He also sent a eunuch from Yan named Zhonghang Yue to go along as her tutor. Yue was unwilling to go, but the Han officials forced him. "My going there will bring trouble to the Han," he remarked. After Yue arrived, he surrendered to the Xiongnu, who treated him with great favor.[5]

---

[3]A Chinese subordinate ruler during the Han dynasty.

[4]Payments.

[5]In keeping with his historical method, Sima Qian describes more of Zhonghang Yue's adventures outside China elsewhere in his book. Some of them can be found by consulting the indexes to Burton Watson's translations of *The Records of the Historian* (see Selected Bibliography).

The Xiongnu liked the Han silks and foods [that came with the princess]. Zhonghang Yue then said to them, "The entire population of the Xiongnu nation would not amount to a single province in the Han Empire. The Xiongnu's strength comes from their food and clothing being different from those of the Han. They have no need to admire what the Han have. Now the Xiongnu chief is changing your customs and loves Han things. Therefore, even though China sends no more than a fifth of its goods here, it is captivating the entire Xiongnu nation. From now on, when you receive Han silk clothes, put them on when you ride on horseback through the bushes and brambles. Your robes and leggings will immediately be ripped to shreds, demonstrating that silks are no match for the perfect quality of your leather and fur clothes. Similarly, when you receive any Chinese foods, throw them away, so that your people will know that this nourishment does not suit your lifestyle like your milk and curds do." Zhonghang Yue also taught the chief's assistants to itemize and count the population, the domestic animals, and other goods. . . .

Once when a Han ambassador commented that Xiongnu customs showed no respect for old people, Zhonghang Yue rebuked him by asking, "Do not Han customs dictate that when young men are sent off with the army to do garrison duty on the border, their elderly parents at home willingly give up their warm clothing and the fattiest and best food, so that there will be enough for the troops?" "Yes, they do," the Han ambassador admitted. Then Zhonghang Yue continued, "The Xiongnu people clearly demonstrate that their concern is warfare. Since the old and the weak can no longer fight, the fattiest and best food and drink are naturally directed to the strong and healthy. The young men therefore willingly fight to defend the nation, so both fathers and sons are able to live as long lives as possible. How can you say that the Xiongnu look down on elderly people?"

The Han ambassador then said, "Among the Xiongnu people, fathers and sons sleep together in the same tent. When a father dies, the sons marry their own stepmothers, and when brothers die, the other brothers marry their widows! People like this are ignorant of the elegant protocols of headgear and sashes[6] and of procedures at court!"

To this Zhonghang Yue responded, "According to Xiongnu customs, the people consume meat and milk from their domestic animals and wear their hides as clothing, with the animals moving from place to place according to the season to eat grass and drink water. Therefore,

---

[6]These items of clothing indicated the social rank of the person wearing them.

during hard times the men practice on horseback and with their bows, while during easy times they relax, enjoy themselves, and have nothing they have to do. Their laws are simple and easy to follow, the relationship between ruler and subject is untroubled, and the running of the nation is like a man running his family. When fathers and brothers die, they marry the widows to make it hard for the family to die out. Therefore, the Xiongnu, even when times become chaotic, will certainly preserve their families.

"Now, the Han people do not take over widowed wives from fathers and brothers, but relatives become estranged and even kill each other, to the extent of betraying the family and even the dynasty. In addition, protocols and procedures make the hierarchical ranks in society resent each other, and they exhaust themselves working on permanent houses and buildings. They obtain food and clothing by farming and cultivating mulberry trees.[7] They defend themselves by building walled cities, which means that they do not practice defense for war emergencies and become lazy whenever crises are over. Oh, you [Han] mud-hut dwellers, don't waste your words! Even though you talk aggressively, you just can't let your clothes or hats get messed up for a minute! What's the use of that?"

Ever after, when Han ambassadors wanted to extend their speeches, Zhonghang Yue would always squelch them by saying, "Han ambassador, no more talk! Just make sure that your gifts of food and clothing are plentiful enough and of decent quality. You need say no more! And the stuff you bring had better be good, or otherwise we will send horsemen to destroy your autumn harvest." Day and night he helped the Xiongnu chief see opportunities to take advantage of the Han. . . .

[In 162 BCE], Emperor Wen sent a messenger with a letter to the Xiongnu that read:

The emperor respectfully asks about the health of the chief of the Xiongnu. Your ambassadors, the household administrator, and the official Diao Qunan and the palace assistant Han Liao have brought us two horses. We accept them with respect.

In accordance with what the previous emperor decreed, the chief of the Xiongnu was to command the region north of the Great Wall, where men shoot arrows from their bows, while we were to rule the region south of the wall, where the people live in houses and wear hats and sashes. Under this arrangement, the multitudes of inhabitants of these areas would get their food and clothing by farming,

---

[7]Mulberry leaves were used to feed silkworms.

weaving, or hunting, fathers and sons would live side by side, rulers and officials would both be safe, and no one would act violently or rebel. We have heard, however, that a number of evil and deluded men, whose greed for wealth has overcome them, have forsaken justice and broken our peace treaty, paying no heed to what will happen to the multitudes of inhabitants and destroying the harmony that has been in place between the rulers of our two lands.

This, however, is now past history. You said in your [earlier] letter to me that, since our two nations have been brought together again in peace and our two rulers are again in agreement, you want to rest your army and let your horses graze, so that there may be prosperity and happiness for generation upon generation, and so that we can begin again to exist peacefully and harmoniously. We enthusiastically agree with what you said. The sagely wise man, it is said, renews himself every day, reforming and starting over again so that the elderly can rest and the young can mature, with each one keeping his life secure and living out the span of time that Heaven bestows on him. As long as we and the chief of the Xiongnu join together to walk this path, obeying the will of Heaven and having mercy on the people, granting the benefits of peace to generations without end, then no one in the entire world will fail to benefit.

Our two great nations, the Han and the Xiongnu, exist next to one another. Since the Xiongnu live in the north, where the country is cold and the severe frosts arrive early in the year, we have ordered our imperial officials to send annually to the chief of the Xiongnu a specified amount of grain, yeast, gold, silk cloth, thread, fiber stuffing for clothing, and other items.

The world currently is experiencing a secure peace, and our peoples are undisturbed. We and the chief of the Xiongnu must be like their parents. When we look back at the past, we recognize that the plans of our officials came to nothing as a result of minor things and insignificant causes. Nothing of this sort deserves to overturn the concord existing between brothers.

We have heard it said that Heaven is impartial in protecting human beings and that Earth is also unbiased in supporting them. Therefore, we, in company with the chief of the Xiongnu, should dismiss these minor things from the past and walk the great path together. We are obliterating past evils and making plans for the long-term future, so that our two nations' peoples can be united like the sons in a single family. In that way, there will be nothing that cannot be at peace and gain benefits and safety from danger— whether it is the uncountable multitudes of the people, the fish and turtles here below, or the birds that soar above us, indeed whatever walks, breathes, or crawls.

It is the way of Heaven to permit people to come and go freely. Let us both forget the matters of the past. With this in mind, we have given pardons to those who have come to us willingly or became prisoners of war. It is hoped that the chief of the Xiongnu will not blame Zhang Ni and the others like him [who came to us]. We have heard that ancient rulers proclaimed their promises openly and, once they had reached an agreement, never broke their word. The chief of the Xiongnu should take this to heart, so that the entire world can have secure peace. Once a peace treaty has been made, the Han will not be the first to break it! The chief of the Xiongnu should pay special attention to these matters!

When the Xiongnu chief replied that he was ready to agree to the peace treaty, Emperor Wen dictated an edict to the imperial secretary.

[The rest of this chapter describes how the Xiongnu chief at the time agreed to the peace treaty and then how the agreement later fell apart, leading to a resumption of hostilities.]

The Grand Astrologer comments: When Confucius wrote the *Spring and Autumn Annals*, he was very clear in his description of Yin and Huan, dukes of Lu. When he treated the later periods of Dukes Ding and Ai, he wrote much more subtly. Since in this second case, he was writing about his own times, he did not declare his judgment frankly, instead employing subtle and indirect language. The problem with the usual type of people who currently discuss Xiongnu affairs is that they are only interested in acquiring some short-term gain, stoop to any level of flattery to get their opinions accepted, and pay no attention to what the effects might be on everyone concerned. In the meantime, the generals and military leaders who rely on the huge extent and strength of China become bolder and bolder, and the ruler makes decisions according to what they advise. For this reason, they do not have far-reaching accomplishments.

The ancient emperor Yao was certainly wise, but he did not have genuine success as a ruler. The nine regions of the nation had to wait until the reign of Emperor Yu truly to experience peace. To establish a dynasty of true worth, like the honored ones of the ancient times, nothing, I say, is more important than choosing the correct generals and ministers! Nothing, I say, is more important than choosing the correct generals and ministers!

A Chronology of the Life of Herodotus and Events in His *Histories* (560–ca. 414 BCE)[1]

560– 546	Reign of Croesus, king of Lydia; his story opens Herodotus's work.
546	Croesus overthrown by Cyrus, founder of the Persian Empire.
499– 479	Persian Wars; these wars are the main subject of Herodotus's work.
490	Battle of Marathon, near Athens; first Greek defeat of Persian forces.
ca. 484*	Herodotus, Greece's first great historian, born in Halicarnassus, on the southwestern coast of what is today Turkey.
480	Persian king Xerxes invades Greece, inspiring thirty-one Greek states to form a temporary alliance to fight for their political freedom.
	Three hundred Spartans die at the Battle of Thermopylae, which becomes a symbol of the Greek dedication to freedom.
	Greek navy defeats the much larger Persian navy in the Battle of Salamis.
480s– 460s*	Herodotus and his family forced into exile after opposing tyranny in Halicarnassus.
478	Athens takes leadership of Greece from Sparta and establishes a naval alliance that leads to the "Athenian empire" in the Aegean Sea region.
470s*	Athenian naval alliance drives the last remaining Persian outposts from the Aegean Sea region.
450s*	Herodotus begins his travels around the Mediterranean.

[1]An asterisk indicates that the date or dates given for certain events or facts of Herodotus's life and times have been estimated because no documented records providing specific dates exist.

445* Herodotus reportedly wins a prize for performing his history writing before a public audience in Athens.

431– 404 Peloponnesian War between Spartan alliance and Athenian alliance; the war's violence devastates Greece.

ca. 420s* Herodotus finishes his *Histories*.

ca. 414* Herodotus dies.

A Chronology of the Life of Sima Qian and Events in His *Records of the Historian* (551–ca. 86 BCE)

551–479	Life of Confucius, China's most famous philosopher, whose ideas on the moral purpose of history influenced Sima Qian.
227	Jing Ke makes a failed attempt to assassinate the king of Qin (the future First Emperor of Qin).
221	First Emperor of Qin unifies China by force and founds the Qin dynasty.
209–174	Reign of Maodun, chief of the Xiongnu.
206	Han dynasty replaces the Qin Dynasty and remains in power during Sima Qian's life.
188–180	Reign of Empress Lü, famous for her ruthlessness.
ca. 145	Sima Qian born near Longmen, China.
141–87	Reign of Emperor Wu, whom Sima Qian served.
ca. 125	Sima Qian travels extensively in China.
111	Emperor Wu sends Sima Qian on a mission to reorganize imperial territory.
110	Sima Qian's father, Sima Tan, the emperor's Grand Astrologer, dies; asks his son to complete his *Records of the Historian*.
108	Emperor Wu promotes Sima Qian to his father's position as Grand Astrologer.
99	Sima Qian defends his friend, General Li, before Emperor Wu.
98	Emperor Wu has Sima Qian castrated for alleged disloyalty.
ca. 91	Sima Qian writes to Ren An explaining why he did not commit suicide.
ca. 86	Sima Qian dies.

Questions for Consideration

1. What themes concerning how to live one's life emerge from Herodotus's story of Croesus (Document 1)?

2. What do you think Herodotus's Greek audience would have thought of his descriptions of how others lived (Document 2), especially his representation of the customs of the Persians, who were the enemies of the Greeks in the war that he makes the major subject of his history?

3. Why do you think Herodotus devotes so much attention to King Xerxes' building a bridge to bring his army across the channel separating Asia and Europe (Document 3)?

4. Were considerations of strategy or honor more important in motivating the three hundred Spartans to fight to the death at Thermopylae (Document 4)?

5. In what ways is Artemisia's gender relevant to the significance of her actions as a Persian commander and royal adviser (Document 5)?

6. What should be the role of the historian in presenting information about divine intervention in human life, as in the story of Hermotimus (Document 5)?

7. Do you think it is more effective for a work of history to end with an explicit conclusion or to end the way that Herodotus's *Histories* does (Document 6)?

8. According to Sima Qian's letter to Ren An (Document 7), what motives and rewards justified the personal sacrifice he endured to finish writing *The Records of the Historian*?

9. Based on Sima Qian's narrative, what judgment does he suggest about the actions of the First Emperor of Qin (Document 8)?

10. What purpose do legendary stories, such as the birth of Gaozu (Document 9), serve in national histories?

11. What characteristics allowed Empress Lü to exercise power in early imperial China (Document 10)?

12. What were Bo Yi and Shu Qi trying to achieve with their resistance to the emperor (Document 11)? Is it reasonable to call them martyrs? If so, martyrs for what cause?

13. What do you think is portrayed as the proper relationship between codes of conduct in peacetime and in war in the philosophies of war attributed to Sun Wu and Sun Bin (Document 12)?

14. Do you think that later Chinese scholars were justified in criticizing Sima Qian for including stories such as that of the assassin Jing Ke (Document 13)?

15. What characteristics of the Xiongnu seem most important in Sima Qian's account (Document 14)? Why do you think he emphasizes these particular characteristics?

16. What do you think it is possible to learn by comparing two historians from very different times and places?

17. What are the most notable differences and similarities between the approaches to writing history of Herodotus and Sima Qian?

18. Do Herodotus and Sima Qian deal differently with the challenge of being objective in the presentation of evidence while at the same time expressing subjective interpretations of events and people's motivations?

19. Why do you think both Herodotus and Sima Qian include significant discussions of "others" and their ways of life?

20. Do you think Herodotus and Sima Qian agree on the importance of individuals in influencing the course of history?

21. Why do you think Herodotus and Sima Qian present the role of divine power in history in the ways that they do?

22. How would you compare Herodotus's and Sima Qian's descriptions of the ways rulers exercise power?

23. Do you think Herodotus and Sima Qian express or imply similar moral judgments of human character and actions?

Selected Bibliography

HERODOTUS: TRANSLATIONS

De Sélincourt, Aubrey, trans. *Herodotus: The Histories*. Revised by John Marincola. London: Penguin Books, 1996.

Grene, David, trans. *Herodotus: The History*. Chicago: University of Chicago Press, 1987.

Macaulay, G. C., trans. *Herodotus: The Histories*. Revised by Donald Lateiner. New York: Barnes & Noble Classics, 2004.

Strassler, Robert B., ed. *The Landmark Herodotus*. New York: Pantheon Books, 2007.

Waterfield, Robin, trans. *Herodotus: The Histories*. Oxford: Oxford University Press, 1998.

HERODOTUS: STUDIES

Bakker, Egbert J., Irene J. F. de Jong, and Hans van Wees, eds. *Brill's Companion to Herodotus*. Leiden: Brill, 2002.

Dewald, Carolyn. Introduction. In *Herodotus: The Histories*, trans. Robin Waterfield. Oxford: Oxford University Press, 1998.

Dewald, Carolyn, and John Marincola, eds. *The Cambridge Companion to Herodotus*. Cambridge: Cambridge University Press, 2006.

Harrison, Thomas. *Divinity and History: The Religion of Herodotus*. Oxford: Oxford University Press, 2000.

Lateiner, Donald. *The Historical Method of Herodotus*. Toronto: University of Toronto Press, 1989.

Munson, Rosaria Vignolo. *Telling Wonders: Ethnographic and Political Discourse in the Work of Herodotus*. Ann Arbor: University of Michigan Press, 2001.

Romm, James. *Herodotus*. New Haven, Conn.: Yale University Press, 1998.

Thomas, Rosalind. *Herodotus in Context: Ethnography, Science and the Art of Persuasion*. Cambridge: Cambridge University Press, 2000.

SIMA QIAN: TRANSLATIONS

Dawson, Raymond, trans. *Sima Qian: Historical Records*. Oxford: Oxford University Press, 1994.

Markely, J. "Awards of Fiefdoms in the Reign of Emperor Wu-di: A Translation and Commentary of *Shiji* Chapter 20 Chronological Table 8." *Zentralasiastische Studien* 32 (2003): 35–99.

Nienhauser, William H., Jr., ed. *The Grand Scribe's Records*. Bloomington: Indiana University Press, 1994–2006. Vol. 1, *The Basic Annals of Pre-Han China by Ssu-ma Ch'ien*; vol. 2, *The Basic Annals of Han China by Ssu-ma Ch'ien*; vol. 5.1, *The Hereditary Houses of Pre-Han China, Part 1*; vol. 7, *The Memoirs of Pre-Han China by Ssu-ma Ch'ien*.

Watson, Burton, trans. *Records of the Grand Historian of China: Translated from the Shih Chi of Ssu-ma Ch'ien*. Vol. 1, *Early Years of the Han Dynasty, 209 to 141 BC*. New York: Columbia University Press, 1961.

———. *Records of the Grand Historian of China: Translated from the Shih chi of Ssu-ma Ch'ien*. Vol. 2, *The Age of Emperor Wu, 140 to circa 100 BC*. New York: Columbia University Press, 1961.

———. *Records of the Historian. Chapters from the Shih Chi of Ssu-ma Ch'ien*. New York: Columbia University Press, 1969.

———. *Records of the Grand Historian: Qin Dynasty*. Hong Kong: Chinese University of Hong Kong and Columbia University Press, 1993.

———. *Records of the Grand Historian: Han Dynasty, 2 volumes*. Rev. ed. Hong Kong: Chinese University of Hong Kong and Columbia University Press, 1993.

SIMA QIAN: STUDIES

Benjamin, C. *The Yuezhi: Origin, Migration and Conquest of Northern Bactria*. Turnhout, Belgium: Brepols, 2007.

Cao, Lei. *The Terracotta Army of Emperor Qin Shi Huang*. Beijing: Foreign Languages Press, 2000.

Durrant, Stephen W. *The Cloudy Mirror: Tension and Conflict in the Writings of Sima Qian*. Albany: State University of New York Press, 1995.

Hardy, Grant. *Worlds of Bronze and Bamboo: Sima Qian's Conquest of History*. New York: Columbia University Press, 1999.

Hardy, Grant, and Anne Behnke Kinney. *The Establishment of the Han Empire and Imperial China*. Westport, Conn.: Greenwood Press, 2005.

Lévy, André. *Chinese Literature, Ancient and Classical*. Translated by William H. Nienhauser, Jr. Bloomington: Indiana University Press, 2000.

Lewis, Mark Edward. *The Early Chinese Empires: Qin and Han*. Cambridge, Mass.: Harvard University Press, 2007.

Loewe, Michael. *A Biographical Dictionary of the Qin, Former Han and Xin Periods, 221 BC–AD 24*. Leiden: Brill, 2000.

———. *The Men Who Governed Han China: Companion to* A Biographical Dictionary of the Qin, Former Han and Xin Periods. Leiden: Brill, 2004.

Twitchett, Denis, and Michael Loewe, eds. *The Cambridge History of China*. Vol. 1, *The Ch'in and Han Empires, 221 BC–AD 220*. Cambridge: Cambridge University Press, 1986.

Watson, Burton. *Ssu-ma Ch'ien: Grand Historian of China.* New York: Columbia University Press, 1958.

Wilkinson, Endymion. *Chinese History: A Manual.* Rev. ed. Cambridge, Mass.: Harvard University Asia Center for the Harvard-Yenching Institute, 2000.

COMPARATIVE HISTORY AND HISTORIOGRAPHY

Ferguson, John, and Milton Keynes. "Early Contacts between China and the West" and "The Evidence of the Ancient Geographers," Parts I and II of "China and Rome." In *Aufstieg und Niedergang der römischen Welt,* vol. II.9.2, ed. Hildegard Temporini, 581–85. Berlin: Walter de Gruyter, 1978.

Lloyd, G. E. R. *The Ambitions of Curiosity: Understanding the World in Ancient Greece and China.* Cambridge: Cambridge University Press, 2002, esp. chap. 1, "Histories, Annals, and Myths."

Prusek, Jaroslav. "History and Epics in China and the West." In *Chinese History and Literature. A Collection of Studies,* 17–34. Dordrecht, Holland: D. Reidel, 1970.

Schaberg, David. "Travel, Geography, and the Imperial Imagination in Fifth-Century Athens and Han China." *Comparative Literature* 51 (1999): 152–91.

Schwartz, Benjamin. "History in Chinese Culture: Some Comparative Reflections." *Chinese Historiography in Comparative Perspective: History and Theory* 35 (1996): 23–33.

Shankman, Steven, and Stephen W. Durrant. *Early China/Ancient Greece: Thinking through Comparisons.* Albany: State University of New York Press, 2002.

———. *The Siren and the Sage: Knowledge and Wisdom in Ancient Greece and China.* London: Cassell, 2000.

Teng, S. Y. "Herodotus and Ssu-ma Ch'ien: Two Fathers of History." *East and West* 12 (1961): 233–40.

Index

Abrocomes, 70
Abydos
   bridge across Hellespont from, 53–55
   Greek advance into, 81
   Xerxes' advance into, 53–54, 55, 56–57
Adrastus, 38–41
Aeginetans, 63, 74
Aeolians, 32, 81
Ahura Mazda, 46*n*
Alcaeus, 32
Alpheus, 70
Alyattes, 32, 34
Amasis, king of Egypt, 35
Amestris, 79–80, 81
Amphictyons, 66, 71
Analects (Confucius), 15
ancestors, importance of not shaming, 90
Apollo, 43, 45
Arabia, 47
Archilochus, 34
Aristodemus, 71–72
Artabanus, advice to Xerxes, 57–60
Artayktes, 54, 82–83
Artaynte, 79–80
Artayntes, 79
Artembares, 83
Artemisia
   advice to Xerxes, 76–77
   as fleet commander, 73, 74, 75
Art of War, The (Sun Bin), 118
Art of War, The (Sun Wu), 115
"Arts of War: The Biographies of Sun Wu
   and Sun Bin" (Sima Qian), 115–19
assassins, 120–28
Assyria, 47
Astyages, 41, 46
Athenades, 66
Athens
   Battle of Salamis and, 73, 74–75
   naval alliance of, 139–40
   Peloponnesian War and, 3, 140
   Persian Wars and, 4, 63
   prosperity of, 26
   siege of Sestos and, 81–83
   Solon and, 35
   Xerxes' burning of, 73, 76

Atys, 37–41
audience, responsibility for making connections, 11, 24, 27

Babylonia, intellectual achievements in, 5
Ban Gu, 85
barbarian cultures. *See* "others" cultures
Bian Sui, 113
Biton, 35–36
"Born from a Dragon: The Origins of Gaozu,
   Founder of the Han Dynasty" (Sima
   Qian), 101–5
Bo Ya, 86
Bo Yang, 25
Bo Yi, 86, 113–14, 115

Candaules, king of Lydia, 32–34
Cao Mo, 124
castration
   Hermotimus's revenge of, 77–78
   as "palace punishment," 86
   shame and disgrace of, 86–87, 90
   of Sima Qian, 16–17, 85–86, 89–90
   See also eunuchs
"Castration as the Price of Writing History:
   Sima Qian's Autobiographical Letter to
   Ren An" (Sima Qian), 85–93
Chen Ping, 108–9
Chersonese, 81, 82, 83
China
   destruction of history books and scholars,
     13, 100
   dynastic histories, 25–26
   establishment of Qin dynasty, 13, 14, 27,
     94–100
   Han dynasty, 13, 27
   history writing before Sima Qian, 17–19
   moral aspect of history writing in, 18–19,
     24–26, 28
   women's roles in, 20
chronologies
   of Ionian historians, 6
   of later Greek historians, 9
   Spring and Autumn Annals, 18
   vs. Herodotus's nonlinear style, 8
Chun Yu Yue, 99

147